G000253185

The Manly Book of Poems for Men: A
Practical Guide to Life, Love and Flat-Pack
Furniture Assembly from the World's
Greatest Poets

David Craig and Stephen Craig

David Craig is a retired lecturer in English with a Master's Degree in Modern Literature in English. He has taught for over thirty years in the Further Education sector and has attempted to make English Literature relevant to engineers, building tradesmen and biochemists. He now amuses himself by writing short stories, rambling over mountains and living a life of freedom, tranquillity and leisure.

Stephen Craig is a Science Writer with a PhD in Animal Behaviour. He has written academic articles in the fields of Medicine and Biotechnology and leads a clandestine, semi-amphibious life as a health and fitness blogger, Dr Mudskipper. Stephen's mission is to summarize and share the best bits of Science and Art (often injecting a little performance-enhancing irreverence between their toes) in order to inspire people to lead happier, healthier lives. In his spare time, Stephen is an amateur triathlete, obstacle-race fetishist and scone enthusiast.

Comments from reviewers and press:

"A light-hearted and modern take on a selection of classic poetry" – *Belfast Telegraph*

"Humorous and educational. Should be in every toilet in every house for those quiet moments of reflection" – John Toal, *Radio Ulster*

To our frabjous family: Linda, Connie, Sarah, Anthony, Max and Isabel

"A little nonsense now and then is relished by the wisest men" – Roald Dahl

Contents

Part 4. Love and Loss: Lessons in love from the Chat-Up Merchant of Venice and friends

Part 5. Nature: Not just 'a place where large numbers of ducks fly by overhead uncooked'[1]

---

[1] Stolen from Oscar Wilde.

Preface

David Craig

To our knowledge *The Manly Book of Poems for Men* is the world's first 'macho' self-improvement poetry book; a compilation and explanation of some of the best poems ever written, rebooted and pimped-out for the people least likely to encounter their wisdom, Manly Men.

Having taught poetry and English Literature for more years than I care to remember, I have developed the dark art of 'manning-up' my analyses in order to stimulate the interest of poetry-proof students, men in particular. These skills have been sharpened by a 30 year battle to convince my son that poetry matters. In the end it appears that the trick is to pretend that it does not.

I am in that rare demographic of humanity that understands and loves poetry, yet is prepared to make fun of it in order to share its wisdom with a potentially hostile audience. Together with my son, I have developed a style that treats Shakespeare and Co. with a bit of manly banter, without losing the significance of their work.

If poets are "the unacknowledged legislators of the world", then this book aims to make them a bit more acknowledged by the people who think they are the real legislators...The Manly Men.

Stephen Craig

Throughout my life, I have always appreciated poetry for reasons noble or otherwise. As I was growing up, dad always said that

'Shakespeare puts food on the table'. I quickly did the maths and realized that if this were true, Shakespeare also put new video-game cartridges in my Sega MasterSystem and stinky football boots at the bottom of my gym bag. So I always had a grudging respect for Billy Shakes and thought twice about making fun of his silly wee beard and frilly collar.

Later in school, I wasn't particularly good at English and was forced to roam the corridors as an art student trapped inside the body of a science geek; however, I quickly realized that girls were more interested in *Romeo and Juliet* than deoxyribonucleic acid (DNA), so I would sneak into dad's library and copy out verses of Auden and Keats on to Valentine's Day cards, without really knowing what the words meant. These love poems were always suspiciously easy to find: always within easy reach and carefully bookmarked. (Thanks dad!).

It was only when dad retired and I was living abroad for several years that I really began to appreciate poetry and all it had to offer. Any time I was feeling lonely, uncertain about the future or raging about the locals immunity to my Irish 'charm', dad would offer a gruff, 'You'll be all right, son' followed by an email containing a relevant poem, along with an easy-to-understand explanation of what it was all about. These explanations were a revelation to me; they transformed beautiful and bewildering poems into sound advice and gave me that warm fuzzy glow (or smug satisfaction) of feeling a bit smarter than most blokes, who didn't read poetry.

The poems and knowledge that dad shared with me are too good to keep to ourselves, so we have decided to share them with all the Manly Men out there who aren't 'fortunate' enough to have an English Literary guru as a father. We have worked together to develop a humorous and practical manterpretation of some of the world's greatest poems, so that they can motivate and inspire men everywhere to lead manly lives.

It is our sincere hope that *The Manly Book of Poems for Men* is an accessible and socially acceptable interpretation of poems for men who previously had to hide their poetry books within the pages of a porn mag in order to avoid drawing embarrassing attention to themselves.

Part 1. How to Lead a Good Life: Kicking the black dog and other inspirational advice

Ode on Melancholy

John Keats

Every now and then, even the manliest of Men can slip into a rare bout of melancholy, as economic crises, job insecurity, heartbreak, and the depressing success of the *Fifty Shades of Grey* saga, inevitably take their toll. The truth is that modern living is stressful. Each day we are faced with the relentless pressure to meet the expectations placed upon us by society or aspire to unrealistic goals set by the media and advertisements. We wrestle with difficult philosophical choices, such as the beer-versus-rock-hard-ab dichotomy and the mind-body problem, which can drag the unwary down into an existentialist funk. In this poem, John Keats offers advice on how to cope with sadness and stave off depression.

Keats reminds us that the Manly Man refuses to wallow in self-pity, does not run away from his problems and will never *'let the death-moth be his mindful Psyche'* (seriously, you'll never catch him doing that). No, the Manly Man taps Melancholy on the shoulder, bares his teeth, and goes *"Grrrrr!"* John Keats was one such man, and with this poem he urges us to face melancholy, meditate upon it, and stare the bugger down!

Ode on Melancholy

No, no, go not to Lethe, neither twist
Wolf's-bane, tight-rooted, for its poisonous wine;
Nor suffer thy pale forehead to be kiss'd

By nightshade, ruby grape of Proserpine;
Make not your rosary of yew-berries,
Nor let the beetle, nor the death-moth be
Your mournful Psyche, nor the downy owl
A partner in your sorrow's mysteries;
For shade to shade will come too drowsily,
And drown the wakeful anguish of the soul.

But when the melancholy fit shall fall
Sudden from heaven like a weeping cloud,
That fosters the droop-headed flowers all,
And hides the green hill in an April shroud;
Then glut thy sorrow on a morning rose,
Or on the rainbow of the salt sand-wave,
Or on the wealth of globed peonies;
Or if thy mistress some rich anger shows,
Emprison her soft hand, and let her rave,
And feed deep, deep upon her peerless eyes.

She dwells with Beauty—Beauty that must die;
And Joy, whose hand is ever at his lips
Bidding adieu; and aching Pleasure nigh,
Turning to poison while the bee-mouth sips:
Ay, in the very temple of Delight
Veil'd Melancholy has her sovran shrine,
Though seen of none save him whose strenuous tongue
Can burst Joy's grape against his palate fine;
His soul shalt taste the sadness of her might,
And be among her cloudy trophies hung.

Stanza 1

No, no, go not to Lethe, neither twist…Wolf's-bane, tight-rooted, for its

13

poisonous wine;…Nor suffer thy pale forehead to be kiss'd…By nightshade,
ruby grape of Proserpine;…Make not your rosary of yew-berries,…Nor let
the beetle, nor the death-moth be…Your mournful Psyche, nor the downy
owl…A partner in your sorrow's mysteries;…For shade to shade will come
too drowsily,…And drown the wakeful anguish of the soul.

Ode on Melancholy is written in three stanzas [2] with ten lines in each.
As your poetic (yet manly) eye will have noticed, the first of these
stanzas is one long sentence. Perhaps this is appropriate as the
mood of melancholy is like a long sentence that seems to go on
forever. Tedious and boring, melancholy is like the battery of
your i-Pod going dead ten minutes into a half-marathon;[3] it makes
time drag. Melancholy traps you into a long, mournful tangle of
self-reflection and depression; it slows you down and makes it
very hard for you to put on your straw hat, twirl your cane and
tap-dance back and forth across the stage of life.

In the first stanza, Keats presents us with a list of potential
remedies for melancholy. Firstly, we could drink from the river
Lethe, the river of forgetfulness. In Greek mythology's version
of Willy Wonka and the Underworld, the souls of the dead must
sip from the Lethe in order to leave behind all their memories of
this life. The Lethe runs all the way to Hades, where it is guarded
by the Devil's Oompa Loompas; one sip from this river and
melancholy will be forgotten, but not the catchy little songs
recited by the pitch-fork wielding, orange-faced midgets who
flounce about the riverbank.

Another remedy for melancholy is to twist the poisonous
juice from the roots of a plant called '*Wolf's-bane*' to make a kind
of medieval Buckfast wine. The feeling of numbness that follows

---

[2] A stanza is a swanky word that the manterpreter would translate as a 'section'.
[3] Or worse, your little sister's i-pod not going dead ten minutes into a long car journey.

14

a couple of glasses of Buckfast may offer an escape from melancholy, but there is always the chance you may never wake up again (or worse still, you might; the endless sleep is probably preferable to a Buckfast hangover).

Keats' final cure for melancholy is to end it all with a fatal dose of Nightshade; not the sexy, Lycra-clad Nightshade from the 90's TV show *Gladiators* (a dose of whom would be just the ticket for melancholy), but the altogether less sexy poisonous plant that did for Socrates (the famous philosopher and part-time wrestler).

However, Keats advises us not to take any of these easy options and urges us to face up to melancholy. The cowardly way out is alien to the Manly Man. Rather than waste his life, the Manly Man would sooner give it over to some noble cause, such as digging wells in a drought-stricken land or following the 'farewell' tours of aging rock bands, forced to reform because their members invested their money in crack and hookers instead of a pension (e.g. Guns and Roses, The Eagles, Pink Floyd, and New Kids on the Block – watch this space).

Thoroughly decent chap that he is, Keats not only begs us to avoid suicide and drinking ourselves into oblivion, but also warns us not to dwell on thoughts of decay and corruption; neither the destructive *'beetle, nor the death-moth…'* should be our inspiration. Keats also warns us against becoming obsessed with other symbols of doom, such as owls; with their mournful cries, propensity for biting the heads of bats and general harbingery of death, owls are more like Ozzy Osborne than Orville. Death-fixation should be left to the nocturnal activities of pasty-faced

Goths, groping around in the dark for an identity.[4]

After helpfully talking us out of suicide and devil-worship, Keats ends the first stanza on a positive note, saying that it is better to be awake and in a heightened state of anguish than to be numbed into a state of insensibility, in which we no longer experience feeling of any kind at all. Any man who has ever received a full-blown kick in the balls may beg to differ; still, the Manly Man will take that kick, learn from it[5] and chose real life over any cheap imitation of it. He knows that to have no feeling at all is to be dead.

Stanza 2

But[6] when the melancholy fit shall fall…Sudden from heaven like a weeping cloud,…That fosters the droop-headed flowers all,…And hides the green hill in an April shroud;…Then glut thy sorrow on a morning rose,…Or on the rainbow of the salt sand-wave,…Or on the wealth of globed peonies;…Or if thy mistress some rich anger shows,…Emprison her soft hand, and let her rave,…And feed deep, deep upon her peerless eyes.

In the next section, Keats proposes an alternative strategy for dealing with melancholy. When melancholia falls upon us like a sudden rain shower that changes the nature of the landscape and colours our mood, Keats urges us to focus on the sparks of beauty that are still there if we look hard enough; the beauty of the dew-soaked rose or a multi-coloured streak of rainbow

---

4 White make-up is only acceptable on a male if he has the ability to beat the living crap out of anyone who laughs at him…that's the only reason *The Crow* got away with it.
5 Quickly realise that slapping his partner on the arse in public is not good form.
6 Grammatical note: although our English teacher always told us never to start a sentence with 'but', Keats' has sold more poetry books than Mrs Gibson, so we'll take his word for it).

against a gun-metal grey sky. In amongst the sadness and gloom, captured by words like *'fall'*, *'weeping'*, *'shroud'* and *'droop'* (perhaps the saddest word of all), we have words of hope: *'fosters'*, *'green'*, *April'* and *'rainbow'*. These happier words are more commonly associated with springtime: a season of growth, fertility, and chocolate eggs in shiny coloured wrappers; a time when squirrels and rabbits pack up their swimming trunks and head to mammal Mykonos for sexy time. These images contrast with the gloom and introduce a new and positive atmosphere.

On a more intimate level, Keats tells us to focus our mood on the object of our love even *'if thy mistress some rich anger shows'* and is having a 'psycho-hose-beast' moment. Although our lover may be the momentary cause of our sorrow, there is a strength and sense of wellbeing to be found from looking into their eyes. This vindaloo-esque idea of blending pain and pleasure, joy and sorrow, brings us to the final stanza.

Stanza 3

She dwells with Beauty—Beauty that must die;...And Joy, whose hand is ever at his lips...Bidding adieu; and aching Pleasure nigh,...Turning to poison while the bee-mouth sips:...Ay, in the very temple of Delight...Veil'd Melancholy has her sovran shrine,...Though seen of none save him whose strenuous tongue...Can burst Joy's grape against his palate fine;...His soul shalt taste the sadness of her might,...And be among her cloudy trophies hung.

Until now, Keats has been talking about melancholy as a disembodied mood; he has been speaking on the subject of melancholy. However, in the final section of poem, the first letter

17

of Melancholy is capitalized in order to give her human form[7] and she takes her place alongside other moods, emotions and abstract ideas, which have also been personified. Beauty, Joy, Pleasure and Melancholy are transformed into deities that reside in the temple of Delight, where their statues (like those of the Ancient Greek gods) can be worshipped in all their hard-buttocked majesty.

Keats reminds us that beauty will fade with time, joy is fleeting and pleasure can only be tasted briefly before it becomes cloying and sickly (like the third Terry's chocolate orange on Christmas Day). Even as we feel the joy of the salt wave and delight in the pursuit of pleasure, we know that lurking on the other side of happiness, is melancholy. The fact that beauty, joy and pleasure are transient heightens their intensity, which is magnified further when contrasted against melancholy. Veiled in the shadows, Melancholy has the power to intensify the pleasure of those who accept and understand her. So, Melancholy's powers are no less than those of Joy or Pleasure and she deserves her place in the Temple of Delight. The knowledge that the tackle could come in at any moment makes the feeling of running with the ball so much sweeter.

Through this poem Keats teaches us about the importance of melancholy and offers a strategy for coping with it when the darkness descends. The truth is that melancholy serves to heighten our feelings of joy and happiness, by offering a sharp contrast. If we only ever experienced a constant state of happiness, we would become used to it and our feelings of joy

---

[7] Poets often whip out the magical anthropomorphic capital when they want to give an abstract idea human form in order to help us understand it (e.g. Death, Love and Father Christmas).

would be eroded through familiarity and habituation. Like it or not, melancholy brings us back down to earth and offers a contrast against which we can experience future joy.

The Manly Man understands and accepts that melancholy is a part of life; however, rather than dwell on the darkness, he focuses on the activities that bring joy and meaning to his life and the lives of those he cares about. Just as the earth and flowers soak up the rain, the Manly Man sucks up melancholy and uses it to create something worthy. When faced with heartache, strife or a particularly brutal hangover, the Manly Man puts his head down, works all the harder and turns melancholy into a poem, bigger biceps, or a nice new set of shelves.

Manlifesto: The Manly Man doesn't seek out melancholy; however, when it arrives he accepts it because he knows that this melancholy will pass and the world be all the more beautiful for it. Manly Men don't get hangovers, they merely become Manly Monks meditating on the meaning of melancholy.

Reasons for Attendance

Philip Larkin

Now, there are few things more manly than dedicating ourselves to a worthy cause, but not if our dedication comes at the expense of neglecting everything else. This poem is about self-delusion and the tragic irony that the more seriously we take ourselves and our hobbies, the more silly we appear to everybody else. It describes the battle between a young poet's ego and his happiness as he sacrifices present pleasures for future glories.

In this poem, Philip Larkin warns us not to get so wrapped up in our dreams, the future and ourselves, that we forget about reality, the present and those around us. He also tries to convince us that we need not be alarmed when we see a man in a trench coat, Bovril in one hand and binoculars in the other, staring into our bedroom window; it's just an artist observing the rich tapestry of life.

Reasons for Attendance

The trumpet's voice, loud and authoritative,
Draws me a moment to the lighted glass
To watch the dancers - all under twenty-five -
Solemnly on the beat of happiness.

- Or so I fancy, sensing the smoke and sweat,
The wonderful feel of girls. Why be out there?
But then, why be in there? Sex, yes, but what

Is sex? Surely to think the lion's share
Of happiness is found by couples - sheer

Inaccuracy, as far as I'm concerned.
What calls me is that lifted, rough-tongued bell
(Art, if you like) whose individual sound
Insists I too am individual.
It speaks; I hear; others may hear as well,

But not for me, nor I for them; and so
With happiness. Therefor I stay outside,
Believing this, and they maul to and fro,
Believing that; and both are satisfied,
If no one has misjudged himself. Or lied.

Stanza 1

The trumpet's voice, loud and authoritative,...Draws me a moment to the lighted glass...To watch the dancers - all under twenty-five -...Solemnly on the beat of happiness.

The poet casts a lonely figure, walking through silent, dark city streets. Somewhere in the distance music is playing, and the *'authoritative'* voice of a trumpet draws the poet towards a dance hall. It is strange to describe a trumpet as having authority; however, the trumpet does add a certain sense of occasion to proceedings. Played correctly, it is a star-spangled banner of an instrument, loud and hard to ignore, used to play fanfares and herald the entrance of important people; when the trumpet sounds the crowd falls silent and all attention is concentrated on the trumpet-worthy event to come. Played badly, it sounds like a highly amusing trouser accident.[8] It is worth noting that the trumpet was also a popular instrument during the 1950's and 60's (when this poem was written), a dark time when trumpets were abused in the playing of the *Benny Hill* theme tune.

The poet is drawn by the music to a dance hall. He looks through the window that separates him from the popular kids, who dance together *'solemnly on the beat of happiness'*. The dancers are happy, but their dance is solemn; perhaps they are practicing the ridiculous self-conscious, half-arsed dance of the 'cool', attempting to move with an air of superiority and a look of knowing irony that shows that they are above all this...but they're not; none of us are.

Evolutionary biologists reckon that when we throw shapes on the dance floor we are demonstrating to a prospective partner that we are in full working order; that we are healthy and have the potential to be good hunters, child carers, and lovers. So, never have second thoughts about clearing the dancefloor in order to do 'the donut'; you are not being a drunken a**hole; you're just showing off all your good DNA. Dancing is something that you do or you do not; do it properly because half-arsed dancing = half-arsed genes.[9]

Stanza 2

- Or so I fancy, sensing the smoke and sweat,...The wonderful feel of girls.

---

[8] Authoritative as it may be, people may not have taken Bob Dylan quite so seriously had he campaigned for social justice and civil rights on the trumpet. Besides, it is impossible to sing and play the trumpet at the same time (in the case of Dylan, and his new Muppety voice, this may not have been a tragedy, altogether).

[9] The mating ritual is a solemn business; a lot can depend upon it. Get it wrong and you could be stuck raising kids with Paris Hilton (a smashing set of 'teeth' does not a mother maketh).

Why be out there?...But then, why be in there? Sex, yes, but what...Is sex?
Surely to think the lion's share...Of happiness is found by couples — sheer

The poet momentarily feels the desire to join in the dancers' sweaty excitement. He is tempted by the sensual pleasures of sex, drugs and rock'n'roll. The love of music is innate and primal to mankind, and it is hard to resist its spell; anybody whose buttocks do not move of their own volition to 'Superstition' by Stevie Wonder is not to be trusted (and probably an alien, psychopath or both).[10] However, the poet is immune to the powerful combination of smell, touch and sound that whips most of us up into a state of brainless hedonism.

Instead, the young man looking through the glass will keep on over-thinking himself into a state of lonely sobriety. '*Why be out there?*' He does not answer the question, instead he asks the opposite question, '*Why be in there?*' For him the answer seems obvious: sex. Sex is what drives the behaviour of most people. It is the reason we buy swanky watches, acquire gym membership and tight t-shirts (and strive to attain a good working knowledge of poetry). All of these things are weapons in our quest for self-improvement, the pursuit of a noble life, and as much sexy time as possible.

Instead of going in to join the dancers, the poet risks frost bite (and possible arrest) by remaining outside with his face pressed up against the window, thinking sexy thoughts. He asks himself, '*What is sex?*' To be honest, anybody who needs to ask

---

10 But beware, for even the Manliest of feet can start tapping a beat to ABBA songs, even though they ought to know better. This normally happens after a few drinks, when the brain loses some of its control, and the body will seize its opportunity to dance to Shirley Bassey...and possibly *Take That* (depending on how much alcohol has been consumed).

this question is clearly not getting any. Yet, the poet pities the sex-craved trumpet-molesters inside the dance hall; he thinks that they are mistaken in their belief that sex and loving relationships are the key to happiness. The poet wants us to agree with this conclusion; he uses the word '*surely*' in the fourth line of stanza two in order to appeal to our common sense...or maybe he's just trying to reassure himself.

Stanza 3

Inaccuracy, as far as I'm concerned...What calls me is that lifted, rough-tongued bell... (Art, if you like) whose individual sound...Insists I too am individual....It speaks; I hear; others may hear as well,

Most Manly Men would disagree with the poet's perception of sex and companionship in the grand scheme of things. For the poet to describe our view of sex and companionship as an '*inaccuracy as far as [he's] concerned*', makes us question both his reasoning[11] and physical appearance. However, the poet believes that there is another route to happiness, a higher calling than the base pursuit of sex: Art. In his mind's eye, the poet sees himself as a mysterious loner, an outsider observing humanity so that he can educate and dazzle it with his art; everyone else sees a weirdo in an anorak who should probably be kept away from the kids.[12]

---

[11] There is a strong biological argument that the drive to procreate and secure our genetic legacy is the reason behind many strange practices, such as the accumulation of vast sums of little metallic coins and risking physical injury in order to cultivate an image of physical fitness. These enterprises make us happy because we believe they will help us get some loving, not because we're particularly ecstatic about the prospect of reading *Ulysses* or fighting a rugby player who has just thrown a pint over our lover.
[12] Too much solitude can drive people to behave strangely, to engage in displacement activity: an unnatural behaviour that arises as a result of the inability to express a natural

The trumpet that plays to the crowd is not for him. It is a different, special sound that calls him on. The *'lifted, rough tongued bell'*, high in its tower, with its unique sound, represents Art, with a capital 'A'; this is the poet's calling. The bell not only reminds the poet that he is an individual, but *'insists'* upon it. It is this assertion of individuality that sets the poet or artist apart, which makes him an outsider looking in.[13] With these words, Philip Larkin reminds us of his uncanny knack of being able to describe the innermost pretensions of a self-satisfied, smug little gobshite.

Stanza 4

But not for me, nor I for them; and so…With happiness. Therefor I stay outside,…Believing this, and they maul to and fro,…Believing that; and both are satisfied,…If no one has misjudged himself. Or lied.

And so the poet stays on the outside looking in, an objective observer unsullied by the smoke, sweat and sex. The poet's belief in what he says is like the belief in a high religious calling. He sees himself as a priest, pure and celibate in the service of Art, giving up carnal pleasure in the pursuit of purity and an afterlife in which his 'good work' on earth will be remembered for generations to come.[14] The poet believes that sacrificing everything for a higher calling makes him happy; and he supposes that the masses are

---

one. These behaviours include pacing of tigers in captivity, self-destructive feather-plucking of caged birds, and golf (or staring at people through the window of a nightclub).

13 Individuality has a lot to answer for; the idea that originality is the essence of good art is the reason that art galleries are gradually replacing paintings of fields and bowls of fruit with sculptures of half a shark's arse made out of diamond studded tampons preserved in formaldehyde, or an effigy of the pope rendered in *Jammie Dodgers* and *Marmite*.

14 It is a risky and un-natural business to sacrifice the present at the expense of the future, which could explain why priests and artists are notorious pissheads and sexual deviants.

content to *'maul to and fro'* like mindless animals, believing that sensual gratification makes them happy. And so each hears their own calling and everyone is happy. They are satisfied.

But is the poet truly satisfied? Has he convinced us that the life of a loner, marching to the sound of a different drum, can be one of fulfilment? That happiness can only be attained through the pursuit of artistic perfection? Has he f@*k! In the final line Philip Larkin pulls the rug out from under his own pretensions. He has a nagging feeling that his beliefs are misplaced. Perhaps he has been living a lie in order to rationalise his intellectual snobbery and social inadequacy; perhaps he is just trying to convince himself that he is happier in his ivory bell tower of lifted values, rather than getting his hands dirty and his ego bashed in the merry dance of humanity.

Whatever we are left thinking, this poem is a work of art written by an individual whose sense of self-doubt allows us to share, with an amused smile, this self-deprecating blast at his own pretensions. And that is why, even though it was a close call, Larkin is a genius, and not, as posited earlier, a smug, self-satisfied little twat.

In this poem, Philip Larkin makes fun of people who take themselves too seriously and life not seriously enough: CEOs and priests who sacrifice family for career progression; amateur athletes who sacrifice having a few beers with friends for a few seconds off their personal best (what's the point if you have no mates to cheer you on); and writers of *Manly Books of Poetry for Men* who sacrifice the first half of the rugby in order to write this sentence.[15] This poem warns us not to get carried away with our

---

[15] We did go and watch the second half though.

own self-importance and not to sacrifice what is actually important for what we think is important; it's easy to get so wrapped up in ourselves and what we believe to be our 'calling' that we forget to enjoy present pleasures.

The Manly Man knows that a life of meaning and a life of pleasure are not mutually exclusive. He knows that happiness comes from spending time doing activities that have both present and future benefits; stuff that is fun, but actually means something: such as training for a triathlon with friends, doing a sponsored beer-athlon[16] to raise money for the local A&E, or some other shared endeavour, like making babies.

The Manly Man also knows that defining yourself by your hobbies (art, academia, or Christianity) is an act of cowardice; an excuse for not participating in things we know nothing about for fear of looking foolish. The Manly Man loves a bit of folly and knows that he'll miss out on much of life if he defines himself by sheds and shed-related activities. The Manly Man is an expert in experience and throws himself into new and life-threatening situations…like dancing.

Manlifesto: The Manly Man knows that happiness comes from doing things that give his life both meaning and pleasure…like playing with fire extinguishers (to simultaneously make sure that they are fully operational [meaning] and make a mate look like the *Marshmallow Man* from *Ghostbusters* [pleasure]).

---

16 The beer-athlon is comprised of a 10 k run followed by 10 pints. At the time of writing, it looks like the beer-athlon will be approved by the International Olympic Committee by 2020 on the basis that it's less silly than table tennis.

After Apple-Picking

Robert Frost

Although the closest that most Manly Men will ever come to apple-picking is eating a Mr Kipling's or drinking cider, they can all relate to hard work and a commitment to worthy ideas and good deeds. This poem uses apples to represent potential and ideas that sparkle with a golden deliciousness in our mind's eye, calling out to be picked and fulfilled. Each of us, with our unique experiences and environment, conjure up millions of ideas, and it is *we* who decide which are worth pursuing and bringing to fruition. However, it is a sad fact of life that you cannot pick every apple, or fulfil every good intention, no matter how hard you work.

In *After Apple-Picking*, Robert Frost helps us recognize that while it is impossible to act upon every worthy idea or chivalrous impulse, it is enough that we do our best; that we lead full, manly lives and take pride and inner peace from the few things that we have done (the marathons run, sheds built, etc.), rather than beat ourselves up about the many things that we should have done (such as spending more time with our partners and children instead of training for marathons and building sheds).

This poem urges us to lead a life worth reflecting upon in our twilight years. It offers advice on how to bullet-proof ourselves against regret and gives useful instructions on the efficient collection of fruit (it's all about the mind apples, baby!).

After Apple-Picking

My long two-pointed ladder's sticking through a tree
Toward heaven still,
And there's a barrel that I didn't fill
Beside it, and there may be two or three
Apples I didn't pick upon some bough.
But I am done with apple-picking now.
Essence of winter sleep is on the night,
The scent of apples: I am drowsing off.
I cannot rub the strangeness from my sight
I got from looking through a pane of glass
I skimmed this morning from the drinking trough
And held against the world of hoary grass.
It melted, and I let it fall and break.
But I was well
Upon my way to sleep before it fell,
And I could tell
What form my dreaming was about to take.
Magnified apples appear and disappear,
Stem end and blossom end,
And every fleck of russet showing clear.
My instep arch not only keeps the ache,
It keeps the pressure of a ladder-round.
I feel the ladder sway as the boughs bend.

And I keep hearing from the cellar bin
The rumbling sound
Of load on load of apples coming in.
For I have had too much
Of apple-picking: I am overtired

Of the great harvest I myself desired.
There were ten thousand thousand fruit to touch,
Cherish in hand, lift down, and not let fall.
For all
That struck the earth,
No matter if not bruised or spiked with stubble,
Went surely to the cider-apple heap
As of no worth.
One can see what will trouble
This sleep of mine, whatever sleep it is.
Were he not gone,
The woodchuck could say whether it's like his
Long sleep, as I describe its coming on,
Or just some human sleep.

Stanza 1 (Part 1)

My long two-pointed ladder's sticking through a tree...Toward heaven still,...And there's a barrel that I didn't fill...Beside it, and there may be two or three...Apples I didn't pick upon some bough...But I am done with apple-picking now.

On first glance, this poem seems straightforward; it is written in matter-of-fact language that anyone could understand, and there is nothing terribly complicated about picking apples. Poetry-deprived men of questionable manliness will likely presume that this poem has no fancy comparisons, difficult metaphors, or imagery to decipher.[17] Not so the Manly Man, he recognizes a mind-apple when he sees one!

---

[17] We can but pity these fools who wouldn't recognize an allegory, even if they were bitch-slapped by one.

In stanza one, it is as though we are picking apples alongside the poet, and we too are considering the task at hand. We look at the ladder and the unfilled basket. The ladder's points rest securely in the branches of the trees, they point 'toward heaven still'; the word 'heaven' lets us know where the poet's thoughts are leading to. The ladder does not simply point at the sky, but to the paradise that awaits us at the end of our lives when we, like the apples, are harvested. A finger up the nose also points heavenward, but apples, rather than bogeys, offer a more romantic and appropriate symbol for realized dreams and achievements; besides, the legacy of the Manly Man is far too worthy to be rolled between the thumb and forefinger of time, and then flicked into oblivion.

The poet looks around at the practical results his own efforts during the harvest. The barrels are not filled and there are more apples left to be gleaned from the tree. There is more work to be done before the harvest is complete and the poet can be truly satisfied with his work. But satisfied he must be, for he is 'done with apple-picking now'; the poet is tiring, and soon the time for harvesting will be over.

Stanza 1 (Part 2)

Essence of winter sleep is on the night,...The scent of apples: I am drowsing off...I cannot rub the strangeness from my sight...I got from looking through a pane of glass...I skimmed this morning from the drinking trough...And held against the world of hoary grass...It melted, and I let it fall and break...But I was well...Upon my way to sleep before it fell,...And I could tell...What form my dreaming was about to take.

31

Winter is approaching fast and it will soon be time for the poet to rest. In wintertime everything stops; seeds lie dormant and animals hibernate. Everything closes in upon its own resources and prepares to slumber through the cold and frost. The same can be said of life. We grow through the spring and summer of our youth and middle age and then slow down into old age, the creeping winter of our lives; a time, perhaps, for taking stock, for looking back and questioning how we used our time. What was that all about? What did we produce? What did we create? What purpose did we give ourselves and did we succeed in that purpose?

'I cannot rub the strangeness from my sight...I got from looking through a pane of glass.' The poet looks at the world through a sheet of ice on the surface of a drinking trough. From this new and unusual perspective, the familiar appears strange and different. Poets often describe things with a fresh and original eye in order to help us see the truth: in this case, it is the sobering reminder that there will come a time when we are no longer as vital as we are now (when the thought of a threesome will fill us with more dread than excitement).

It all seems terribly depressing, but Robert Frost is warning us against complacency. He is urging us to throw ourselves into worthy pursuits while we have our health and energy, and he dunks our heads in the ice-cold water of the drinking trough in order to shake us from our own lethargy. This poem is a well-intentioned word-wedgie of sorts.[18]

---

[18] Similarly, we have the power to inspire, or depress, those around us. By sharing our perspectives, we can influence the lives of others, making them see the world as a sad, grey approximation of the real thing (if you're a grumpy old git) or helping them to see the world as a vibrant place fizzing with colour, hope and possibility.

Stanza 1 (Part 3)

Magnified apples appear and disappear,...Stem end and blossom end,...And every fleck of russet showing clear...My instep arch not only keeps the ache,...It keeps the pressure of a ladder-round...I feel the ladder sway as the boughs bend.

The poet gathers up his creations and considers his lifetime's work. His achievements become distorted with the passage of time; their importance becomes magnified, exaggerated or else they disappear into insignificance.

In the poet's vision, all the apples he has picked, or left upon the branch, come and go in his mind's eye, like all the poems he has written or left unwritten (or all the sheds he has built or left in their flat pack).[19] Each poem is specific and clear and is the result of hard work. Like picking apples, the effort of creating each poem has left its mark whether it has been written down or not.

Some apples are left on the tree, and the basket remains unfilled; however, the poet must be content with what he has harvested – what he has written. The time for production is over and it is now time for the poet to put on his slippers and count the measure of the harvest with the end of his pipe, until he drifts off to sleep.

Stanza 2 (Part 1)

And I keep hearing from the cellar bin...The rumbling sound...Of load on load of apples coming in...For I have had too much...Of apple-picking: I

---

[19] Robert Frost liked a good shed as much as the next Manly Man.

am overtired…Of the great harvest I myself desired…There were ten thousand thousand fruit to touch,…Cherish in hand, lift down, and not let fall…

In the second part of the poem, just as the poet seems happy to slumber and take a well-earned rest, he can do no such thing. The vision of the apples has melted away but their sound will not let him sleep; he is haunted by the ghost of Granny Smith. The rumbling apples are like the ideas still rolling around in his imagination. Each one could still be taken and used, but it is time to finish with the work of creating and producing. The poet is exhausted; the point has come when the effort is too much and his imagination needs to sleep.

The poet has no sense of regret that some of the harvest remains ungathered. No one has forced him to pick the apples and no one has forced him to pen the words. It was his own desire to make the effort, and each apple, poem, and idea (even the silly one about power-hosing the apples off the trees) is to be appreciated as special and unique.

Stanza 2 (Part 2)

For all…That struck the earth,…No matter if not bruised or spiked with stubble,…Went surely to the cider-apple heap…As of no worth…One can see what will trouble…This sleep of mine, whatever sleep it is…Were he not gone,…The woodchuck could say whether it's like his…Long sleep, as I describe its coming on,…Or just some human sleep.

Even the apples that the poet has rejected took some effort to pick, as did the apples that fell from his grasp, ideas that slipped his ability to give them expression. We have neither the time nor the ability to nurture all of our dreams, and not all of them are worthy of our attentions; these are destined to rot away in the back of our minds like apples left to ferment and moulder away *'in the cider-apple heap'*.

It could well be that the cider bin is the best place for wasted ideas. How better to recycle them than as alcohol, under the influence of which we have had many of our better ideas (and many of our worst)? Although it is a lottery to dunk for ideas with your head dipped in cider, you never know what impulse you might act upon; a practice not without its merits.[20]

Every now and then, it is good to drink away a few ideas and preoccupations, to cast them aside and give yourself a break. Going out on the piss may be more productive than you think. An 'alternative' state of mind may smash together the same old thoughts in a different way. Who knows? You might wake up with some interesting new idea. The fact that it will undoubtedly be shrouded in a dark cloud of pain should not deter you. To extend this line of thought, and refine a logic worthy of Einstein or Yoda: if you drink cider, you feel like shit; shit is fertilizer for seeds of thought; seeds of thought grow into apples of realized ideas (...or into apples that lead to the dark side). So, out of this rotten, decayed, compost of broken ideas, should spring a new crop of even better ones!

No matter how long or short the oncoming *'human sleep'* of the poet's imagination, the danger is that it will be haunted by dreams of what he might have achieved. The poet must be content with the imperfect harvest of his life's work. Now is the time to enjoy it.

---

[20] As the great poet William Blake, friend to all alcoholics, believer in fairies, and an extra literary name to throw into polite conversation, once said, *'The path of excess, leads to the Palace of Wisdom.'* What Manly Man could disagree with such wise sentiment?

This poem reminds us that how we live our life, and what we do with it, will influence the length and the quality of our *old-codgerdom*. We will either face the winter of our lives with regret, or relive the victories and spectacular failures of a life well lead; our snippets of success will be the sparks that keep the cold at bay. Winter will come to us all and it is preferable that it be spent cosily in a mind glowing with worthy memories, than out in the cold of a life poorly led.

We all know pseudo-men who, although young and in their physical prime, are already in the winter of their lives. Some have exhausted their energies in the pursuit of someone else's dream, pawned their ideas for a car, a house and a safe life. They are zombies who shudder along through their lives on automatic pilot, eating, sleeping, occasionally screwing, and always complaining.[21]

Fortunately, as men who are manly, we have the energy, passion and belief to achieve the majority of our good intentions, and still have time left over to consider some of the more dubious. We are in the business of getting shit done and preparing ourselves for a cosy winter, when we will be tucked up in a tartan blanket by the fireside, reliving the highlights in the twilight of our lives: love affairs with Argentine Tango instructors; mountains conquered and oceans braved; worthy foes battled and befriended; brandies and books savoured at sunset; yards of ale downed at dawn; and many sleepless nights spent in the pursuit of a noble and worthy existence.

This poem is a reminder to appreciate this wonderful

---

[21] Other pseudo-men scrump around for the ideas of others; apple-snafflers, who rob jokes and philosophies, passing them off as their own. Such men know nothing of poetry.

moment in your lifetime and to really go for it! Now, look yourself in the mirror! Give your face a slap! Harder! Now, roar!

Manlifesto: The Manly Man does his best to lead a full life that is worth reflecting upon in the twilight of his years; but he understands that it is not possible to follow every dream or complete every good deed. Try not to beat yourself up too much about the things you should have done, and be proud of those things that you did. (Nobody else remembers your penalty miss in the semi-final of the 1987 North Down Boy Scouts football tournament).

On First Looking into Chapman's Homer

John Keats

Now, we're not going to lie to you; it is going to take a Herculean effort to make it through this poem. However, if you can battle through its esoteric references to ancient literature and keep an open mind, you'll see that this is not a work of elitist bullshit intended for the stripy-blazer brigade, but a gateway to Ancient Greece and swashbuckling adventure. This poem is about the first time that Keats read a decent translation of Homer's *Odyssey*. Until that moment, Homer's world of epic battles and heroic deeds was a closed book to most people, including Keats. It's fair to say that Chapman's translation rocked Keats' world; so much so, that he wrote a poem about it.

This poem is a reminder that first impressions can be misleading and that there is much in the world that we do not and cannot know (even if you have a degree in Ancient Greek); however, if we accept these facts with humility, and make a bit of effort to understand the ideas and art of others, we will be inspired more often than we are frustrated. It is also a test of the Manly mind. If you can battle through the text like Jason or one of his Argonaut minions, you'll learn how to beat what appears to be monstrous pretension into a world of inspiration, and learn useful life-skills, such as how to use a shield as a mirror so you don't turn to stone when fighting a woman who has snakes for hair. (This poem will also allow you to add the illustrious name of Homer to your ever-growing list of names and uber-mentionables to drop into polite conversation). So, read on for the inspiration of Homer, translated by Chapman, reflected upon by Keats and digested by us…a bit like that coffee that gets passed through a cat.

On First Looking into Chapman's Homer

Much have I travell'd in the realms of gold,
And many goodly states and kingdoms seen;
Round many western islands have I been
Which bards in fealty to Apollo hold.
Oft on one wide expanse had I been told
That deep-brow'd Homer ruled as his demesne;
Yet did I never breathe its pure serene
Till I heard Chapman speak out loud and bold:
Then felt I like some watcher of the skies
When a new planet swims into his ken;
Or like stout Cortez when with eagle eyes
He star'd at the Pacific - and all his men
Look'd at each other with a wild surmise -
Silent, upon a peak in Darien.

This poem is a sonnet, which is a specific type of poem made up of fourteen lines. In general, the first eight lines of a sonnet put forward an idea or a theme and the last six lines reflect upon what it all means.

Lines 1-8

Much have I travell'd in the realms of gold,…And many goodly states and kingdoms seen;…Round many western islands have I been…Which bards in fealty to Apollo hold.…Oft on one wide expanse had I been told…That deep-brow'd Homer ruled as his demesne;…Yet did I never breathe its pure serene…Till I heard Chapman speak out loud and bold:

On first looking into *On First Looking into Chapman's Homer*, you are met with so much esoteric bollocks that you probably wish you hadn't bothered. The poem is riddled with such archaic language and so many references to Ancient Greece that you might think it had been written solely to show off Keats' knowledge of the classics; however, Keats was just an ordinary (yet Manly) man who had not been taught to read Ancient Greek at public school or university and consequently had never been able to enjoy the heroic battles and half-naked daring-do described by one of History's greatest poets, Homer.

If poetry has the power to transform, then Homer is Optimus Prime. He predates Chaucer, Cervantes and Shakespeare, and his epic poem, *The Odyssey*, has sold even more copies than *The Da Vinci Code* (and not just because it has been in the bookshops for a few thousand years longer).

In the eighteenth and nineteenth centuries, it was popular to read about the legends of antiquity; however, the translations of works in Ancient Greek or Latin were often badly done with the translator relying on other translations.[22] Consequently, Chapman's unpretentious translation of Homer's *Odyssey* (or *Manly translation of Homer for Manly Men*, if you like) was a revelation to Keats. The first eight lines of the poem describe its impact on Keats: the translation whisks him across the expanse of Greek myth and legend. A dead land is brought to life and the taste of this new world saturates Keats' senses, like the opium of which he was fond.

---

[22] In a Victorian equivalent of *Google Translate*.

Keats' imagination takes wing as the words carry him to the fabled world of Ancient Greece; of islands in the Aegean Sea ruled by heroes and gods and nymphos;[23] he feels the heat on his skin and can hear the tales of storytellers, or bards, who were inspired by Apollo. Through Chapman's translation, Keats is able to enjoy the sneaky genius of the Trojan Horse, the adventures of Odysseus and the sacking of Troy (which was not a pornographic interlude); he is captivated by weird and wonderful Gods, like Zeus, Athena, and Apollo, and magical beasts, such as unicorns and all the half-and-halfs: the fabled cockatrice and minotaur and lesser-fabled escargringo (sombrero-wearing snail with flamingo's wings and back to front kneecaps).

We are still inspired and influenced by Homer's tales. Soap opera writers draw their ideas from the Homeric themes of revenge, betrayal, rape, murder, courage, cunning, fortitude, fate and love. An excellent example is that episode of *EastEnders* in which the oracle (Dot Cotton) tells Dirty Den that one of his sons will steal ownership of the Queen Vic Bar. Drawing upon the wisdom of the Greek God, Kronos, Dirty Den takes the only reasonable action available…and eats each of his new-born children. Hollywood continues to mine Ancient Greece for characters (Hercules and Apollo Creed) and ideas for films such as *Clash of the Titans*, *300* and *Jason and the Argonauts*.[24]

Homer's stories of gods and heroes still permeate throughout Western civilization and we are all familiar with them in one form or another. We come across names from Ancient Greece in the Odeon cinemas, and the Apollo theatre. Somebody somewhere

---

[23] The world of Ancient Greece is brought to life and inspires the imagination of the poet, with tales of daring do as legendary as a lad's holiday in Crete, where many *goodly and badly states were seen*, as well as run- ins with beautiful Gods, Goddesses and Minotaurs (their less attractive and over protective friends).

[24] Much superior to its tragiporno sequel: *Alan and the Argonaughty Nympettes*.

thought that Argus, an all-seeing giant with a hundred eyes, would be an appropriate name for a catalogue-based shopping company (Argos). With the name Trojan emblazoned across our packet of condoms, we feel ready to go into inter-gender battle with all the security and success that such a name suggests.[25]

Keats manages to articulate the excitement and joy of experiencing something worthy for the first time. This is not easy to do without swearing; imagine how difficult it would be to describe the thrill of air-guitaring to 'Appetite for Destruction' or giggling through *Life of Brian* for the first time. A theologian (not a musical instrument, but a religious thinker) once said that freedom was a bit like the taste of potatoes. "The first time we taste potatoes," he said, "is also the last time." While we savour a new experience, and our concentration is focused upon it, the intensity of the sensation is quickly lost.[26] Like freedom, new experiences are initially treasured, only to be quickly taken for granted. However, it is clear that Keats does not take Homer's *Odyssey* for granted and this poem captures the joy he felt at understanding it for the first time.

Lines 9-14

Then felt I like some watcher of the skies...When a new planet swims into his ken;...Or like stout Cortez when with eagle eyes...He star'd at the Pacific - and all his men...Look'd at each other with a wild surmise - ...Silent, upon a peak in Darien.

---

[25] Even though the Trojans were tricked into having their barriers breached and took a pasting from Odysseus and his mates.

[26] The same can be said for the first time we ring somebody's doorbell and run away; watching a pensioner stand confused and sad, alone on their doorstep, loses its humour after a while (unless they used to call the police whenever you used their garden gnomes as goalposts when you were a child).

42

In the last six lines of the poem, Keats reflects upon the intensity of *First Looking into Chapman's Homer* and attempts to articulate its significance by comparing it to other monumental events in history, such as the discovery of Uranus by the astronomer Halley, which happened during Keats' lifetime. Think of how amazing it must have been to discover a planet! Never before seen! More amazing still, imagine being allowed to name it after Uranus. God bless Halley, master astrologist and patron saint of toilet humour. Keats also compares his discovery to that of Cortez, the Portuguese explorer, who hacked his way across the Isthmus of Panama (and through most of the Native Indians too) in the sixteenth century, not knowing what he would find. Imagine the impact of knowing that you were the first European to look at the vastness of the Pacific Ocean! In Keats' poem, Cortez and his band of men are awestruck and silenced by the sight. A silence rendered complete by the massacre of anyone who did not understand *"Silencio, por favor."* Reverential silence seems the only appropriate response to such wonder.

And we too, are left in silence at the end of the poem; we are dumbfounded, like Keats upon his discovery of Homer and the wine-dark sea of Ancient Greece. In this poem, Keats has found the words to express the deep emotional and spiritual impact of having the World of Ancient Greece opened up to him – and to think that we were about to dismiss them all as a load of old shite.

On first impressions, this poem appears to have been written by some pseudo-intellectual smartarse, one of the very people that *The Manly Book of Poems for Men* seeks to wrestle poetry away from. However, like us, Keats was actually engaged in the same noble practice of stealing poetry back from the weedy, frilly-cuffed arms of the privileged and putting it back into the hairy-backed hands of the Manlyfolk. This poem serves as a warning against inverse snobbery and disliking that which we don't understand. Just because someone likes Ancient Greek poetry doesn't mean that they don't also like to light their own farts or laugh at cats falling into fish tanks on you tube.

This poem reminds us that it is important to keep an open mind, to listen and allow ourselves to be inspired by advice and ideas of others. There is a misconception that it is not Manly to ask for help; that we are somehow supposed to know the answers to everything, to always be correct. The Manly Man knows that he can't know everything, and that it is tiring and tiresome to pretend that he does. If we don't value any opinion other than our own then we are likely to miss out on good advice and revelatory experiences.[27] The Manly Man is the custodian of curiosity and takes the time and effort to learn from others. This poem is a lesson in manning up, accepting what we do not know, and having the humility and courage to learn from others.

Manlifesto: The Manly Man makes an effort to understand and appreciate the work and ideas of others, rather than dismissing them; unless they're crap... *then* he dismisses them.

---

[27] Who would have believed that Bounty Bars are the secret to a good curry?

Part 2. Humanity: Race, religion and other ridiculous ideas

ygUDuh

E.E. Cummings

ygUDuh is pub poetry. If, as Wordsworth claimed, poetry is the spontaneous overflow of powerful feelings, taking its origin from emotion recollected in tranquillity, then *ygUDuh* is a poem about bar-room bullshit recollected through the haze of a hangover.

This poem was written by E.E. Cummings, an impulsive, manly poet who wrote poetry first and added punctuation later, regardless of the collateral damage done to any full-stops that got in his way. In so much as we can trust a hyphen-molesting, comma deviant and grammar anarchist, this poem has something important to tell us about racism, bladder control and the striking similarities between 'Miss World' and the United Nations.

ygUDuh

ygUDuh (you gotta)
ydoan (you don't)
yunnuhstan (you understand)

ydoan o (you dunno)
yunnuhstand dem (you understand them)
yguduh ged (you gotta get)

yunnuhstan dem doidee (you understand them dirty)
yguduh ged riduh (you gotta get rid of)
ydoan o nudn (you don't know nothing)

LISN bud LISN (Listen bud, listen)
dem (them)
gud (god)
dem (damn)

lidl yelluh bas (little yellow bas-)
tuds weer goin (-tards we're goin)
duhSIVILEYEzum (To civilize them)

Despite the strangeness of the language, there is a boozy sentiment that staggers its way down through this poem which helps us to recognize it as a drunken conversation between a couple of drunken halfwits.

Imagine a crowed bar room in downtown New York. It is 1944 and the country is at war. Japan has struck Pearl Harbour and there is a wave of popular hatred against the 'yellow man'. It is unlikely that any of the New York working men drinking here have ever met any Japanese people, but that is not going to stop them from having a go at them. In the bar, it is difficult to have a normal conversation because of the noise and general hubbub. We catch fragments of a conversation. It is one of those drunken, Saturday-night debates held by people with strong opinions and weak bladders. In their whiskey-addled minds, these people are heroes of philanthropy; representatives on the UN Security Council, only leaving the debate on 'the role of post-war transitional governments,' to have a tactical puke, take a piss, or open international relations with the Polish barmaid.

After a few pints, we all wax lyrical about how politicians favour short-term fixes over fundamental changes that could solve the World's major problems, such as economic crises, immigration, child poverty, and self-service supermarket tills; problems that we have just solved over a few pints...Now, if only we had the hand-eye coordination to write our solutions down on a beer mat, so we could post them to the leaders of the G8 first thing in the morning.

With every beer, the gap in meaning between what we want to say and what we are actually saying stretches further apart. Until:

"Listen here my good man. A system of embargos, backed by the international community, could force the government to make humanitarian changes, or at least ferment discontent in the region."

"I disagree, sir. Any sanctions would only serve to strengthen the hand of the incumbent regime, allowing them to paint the West as the enemy. The only meaningful action is military."

"You mean start a war?"

"No! Back the insurgents. The good, right-thinking people."

"Ah! You mean the ones who will share the oil with us?"

Becomes:

"Listen Bud, listen"
Them
goddam
little yellow bastards
We're goin
To civilize them"

The irony of someone who can hardly speak in joined-up sentences, someone whose views are fundamentally stupid, claiming that they are going to civilize someone else, is both amusing and frightening, and yet woefully common to this day; the denigration of minority groups remains as popular a pastime as it ever was. People are still spouting the same rubbish. Back then it was Germany and Japan; nowadays, the right-wing media prods at the reptilian part of our brain in order to ferment fear of the Muslim community or any non-white beardy person. Papers try to whip up resentment against foreign workers 'stealing our jobs', which we were quite happy to let them do for minimum wage (or a bag of shopping), until the economic crisis came.

Then again, there are people who want to be insulted. The Manly Man can be forgiven for the odd drunken indiscretion, a misjudged racist joke, because he knows that the idea of 'race' is a joke in the first place.[28] Race is a labelling system used by politicians who would dilute our humanity by fragmenting it into the lesser parts of its wonderful whole. These demagogues[29] use fear to create resentment between us and then divide us. In reality, they are the other 'race', a non-human subspecies, recently reclassified as *Homo fuckwit* (a grouping that incidentally also includes climate change sceptics and creationists).

Manly Men know that Manly Mankind all over the World is fundamentally the same. We all want to eat, drink and screw. One of the biological definitions of a species is 'any population of organisms that can interbreed to produce fertile offspring' (sheep-shaggers take note). One only has to consider the annual Miss World competition, and the fact that you would like to

---

28 Besides, the World would be a sadder place if you could not make sheep-shagging jokes at the expense of the Welsh, Kiwis, or any other Sheep-ophilic folk.
29 A demagogue is a bad person, not a place of worship

practice being the same species with any of those women, in order to know that the biologists have got it right...Hmmm, now what are the poets' views on sexism?

Manlifesto: The Manly Man appreciates cultural diversity and identity, but despises narrow-minded nationalism; he knows that at the heart of it all people all around the globe are part of the same glorious species. We all have the same hopes and dreams and we all enjoy the wet, flatulent sound of a freshly-blown raspberry on the back of a loved one's neck.

In Piam Memoriam

Geoffrey Hill

At last! One of those rare things, a poem that actually rhymes! Well, sort of. At least the poet, Geoffrey Hill, makes some sort of effort to begin with, even if the exertion of finding words that sound the same gets a bit too much for him towards the end, where he appears to shrug his shoulders and head off down the pub. But don't let that put you off, for this poem offers great insights into the seedy, silk-dressing-gowned world of Pulp Poetry, and explains how stained-glass effigies had a major impact on the body image of teenagers in medieval times. More than that, this poem encourages us to love Life, warts and all (even the hairy ones).

In Piam Memoriam

Created purely from glass the saint stands,
Exposing his gifted quite empty hands
Like a conjurer about to begin,
A righteous man begging of righteous men.

In the sun lily-and-gold-coloured,
Filtering the cruder light, he has endured,
A feature for our regard; and will keep;
Of worldly purity the stained archetype.

The scummed pond twitches. The great holly-tree,
Emptied and shut, blows clear of wasting snow,
The common, puddled substance: beneath,
Like a revealed mineral, a new earth.

Stanza 1

Created purely from glass the saint stands,...Exposing his gifted quite empty hands...Like a conjurer about to begin,....A righteous man begging of righteous men.

On first glance this poem appears to be little more than a description of the setting for some gothic horror film, with a stained-glass saint standing guard over a bleak, windswept scene. We are given little clue to the backdrop; perhaps it is the leaf-strewn driveway of a neglected church or the kitchen garden of a haunted mansion. It is not initially clear why a religious icon should be the focus of the poem, when a more crowd-pleasing story would be the battle between the chainsaw-wielding lesbian vampires and the sex-crazed zombie swingers going on in the background.[30]

However, the saintly effigy at the centre of this poem suggests that we are in for something a little more worthy. In the first stanza, the saint looks down from the heavenly vantage point of his stained-glass window. Much like a glossy, life-sized poster of 1980's page-three model, Samantha Fox, the saint has been created by obsessed fans using simple materials that are easy to wipe clean. The saint is rendered in mineral glass so pure that light passes through it. The saint looks down at us, his hands open in a gesture of humility; but we can see through him.

The piety that sets the saint apart is not something we can see; he holds his hands out as if to say, "Look! No trickery",

---

[30] Indeed, most attempts at Pulp Poetry have failed; few people remember Edgar Allen Poe's pornographic efforts to spice up *The Raven*: 'As of someone's gigantic knockers upon my bedroom door? "T'is my Sam Fox poster," I muttered, "Sam Foxer's knockers on my chamber door. Only these, and nothing more." For shame, Edgar, for shame.

begging us to believe in his purity. A belief is something we take on trust, something we yearn for to be true; whether it be the saintly piety, or the existence of a partner who will admire our efficient system for recycling underwear over three days. Yet our logical minds tell us such miracles do not operate in the natural world.

Like a Photoshopped poster of Samantha Fox, the glowing effigy of the saint is an unrealistic representation of an ideal that hides all manner of truths. Such heavenly images of purity were the stained-glass Windows™ Photoshop of their day. Colourful and splendid, they offered a superficial, almost supernatural version of the world, with all saintly pimples and pubes airbrushed away. Medieval texts lament how stained glass windows were the primary cause of soul and body-image problems amongst medieval teenagers and weak-minded churchgoers.

Stanza 2

In the sun lily-and-gold-coloured,…Filtering the cruder light, he has endured… A feature for our regard; and will keep;…Of worldly purity the stained archetype.

The stained glass seems to filter *'the cruder [natural] light'* from the sun outside and transforms it into the light of Heaven through the figure of the saint. The image of the saint continues to endure through time. Year after year, the saint has stood patiently beneath the halo of his stained-glass sunburst. He is a symbol of eternal goodness in this less than pure world; someone for us to look up to and take inspiration from.

Stanza 3

The scummed pond twitches. The great holly-tree,...Emptied and shut, blows clear of wasting snow,...The common, puddled substance: beneath,...Like a revealed mineral, a new earth.

Now, in the final stanza we are brought back down from heavenly thoughts to more earthly concerns. Outside in the churchyard, something is moving. The surface of *'the scummed pond twitches'*. What causes the water to move is not clear; it could be the wind or, more likely, the stirrings of life from below the pond's surface. Even though we cannot see through the surface of the scummed pond, we know that there are mysterious and wondrous workings going on below. The leaf mould and loam that coat the surface of the pond offer a sharp contrast to the supernatural purity of the stained-glass saint, but these things have their own kind of beauty, too.

Perhaps Nature herself is better than a sanctified illusion; the dark fluff of a poorly bleached upper lip and subtle whiff of a beautiful, but unwashed, armpit are preferable to a perfume-doused, make-up-splattered ideal.

'The great holly-tree' represents the open church that the righteous turn to, but it is now closed and emptied of any spiritual meaning. The wind blows away the deathly shroud of *'the wasting snow'* and the ice melts into dirty puddles on the common ground that real, unsaintly people walk upon.

The poem finishes with the end of winter. From beneath the dirty scum of the ground's melting surface, the purity of Nature will reveal itself in the wonder of spring and growth. The real and earthy purity of Nature, like mineral gold before it is separated and polished, is contrasted with the superficial, conspicuous purity of the righteous saint. Yet the saint is nothing without the earth; the stained-glass has been manufactured from the same sand and dirt from which the miracle of spring will emerge.

In this poem, Geoffrey Hill reminds us that the everyday wonder of this world is better than a deluded fantasy of the next. The religious and porn-addicted should not objectify their ideal (and both should have more respect for women). Fantastical piety is another kind of smut, and like pornography, it is the last refuge of a wanker. Celebration of fantasy at the expense of the tangible and the real is not just a shame, it is a tragedy. The truth is that there is so much beauty, variety and wonder in the world; so much real life to splash about in. So put on your wellies, wait 'til someone is within splashing distance, and jump in!

Manlifesto: The Manly Man is a spiritual statistician: he hedges his bets and chooses to appreciate and celebrate an imperfect world that he knows to exist over an intangible afterlife that has as much chance of existing as Narnia.

The Second Coming

W.B. Yeats

This poem was written in 1919, and reflects the great political and ideological upheavals of its time; not only were the cataclysmic events of the First World War giving way to mob rule, but Communism and Darwinism were undermining the core values of Christianity. In the shadow of atrocity and uncertainty, people found it difficult to believe in ideas like Freedom, Brotherhood and Love. Ideas that are still under threat today in our increasingly confused world of economic crises, war, and religious fundamentalism.

In times like these, people yearn for certainty and salvation from their strife. Unfortunately, these needs are all too willingly 'met' by various cults and dogma peddlers, such as millennium doomsday merchants, 7th Day Evangelists and Pure Gym. All of these cults offer their followers inner peace, reconciliation of body and soul, and the opportunity to feel superior to everyone else. This poem focuses on one of the most powerful symbols of salvation, the second coming of Christ, when God Jr will deliver his followers from strife and lead them to eternal bliss.

In this poem, W.B. Yeats warns the Manly Man about the dangers of cult, dogma and injecting yourself with too much monkey gland.[31] It offers an alternative vision of what might be in store for us if we subscribe to lives of fundamentalism and

---

[31] W.B. Yeats was a big fan of monkey gland, which was believed to rejuvenate the sexual powers of anyone injected with it.

narrow-mindedness. The second coming of Christ might have less rainbows, more fire and brimstone; less skipping, more fleeing; less clapping, more scalping. Oh, and there is a monster in Stanza two. How cool is that?

The Second Coming

Turning and turning in the widening gyre
The falcon cannot hear the falconer;
Things fall apart; the centre cannot hold;
Mere anarchy is loosed upon the world,
The blood-dimmed tide is loosed, and everywhere
The ceremony of innocence is drowned;
The best lack all conviction, while the worst
Are full of passionate intensity.

Surely some revelation is at hand;
Surely the Second Coming is at hand.
The Second Coming! Hardly are those words out
When a vast image out of Spiritus Mundi
Troubles my sight: somewhere in sands of the desert
A shape with lion body and the head of a man,
A gaze blank and pitiless as the sun,
Is moving its slow thighs, while all about it
Reel shadows of the indignant desert birds.
The darkness drops again; but now I know
That twenty centuries of stony sleep
Were vexed to nightmare by a rocking cradle,
And what rough beast, its hour come round at last,
Slouches towards Bethlehem to be born?

Stanza 1

Turning and turning in the widening gyre...The falcon cannot hear the falconer;...Things fall apart; the centre cannot hold;...Mere anarchy is loosed upon the world,...The blood-dimmed tide is loosed, and everywhere...The ceremony of innocence is drowned;...The best lack all conviction, while the worst...Are full of passionate intensity.

Scary stuff, indeed! The poem is written in two sections; the first is one long sentence made up of eight lines. A falconer releases a falcon from his arm, and the great hunting bird rises into the air, flying in ever widening circles, in search of prey. The function of the falcon is to bring back food that will sustain the falconer; however, as the bird rises higher and higher into the air, it loses contact with the falconer. The falconer represents the main body of ordinary people, while his feathered friend represents the leaders who rise above the masses: rulers whose role should be to provide for their people.

The leaders stray further and further from their people and reality. In some cases they begin to believe that they are the second coming, when the truth is that they probably couldn't even get it up the first time. They leave behind a confused, bewildered, and un-satisfied following; both leaders and congregation have lost their way. *'Things fall apart; the centre cannot hold'*. The sensation is a little like messing about on a roundabout as a child; if you stayed close to the axis in the centre, you could sit tight and observe what was going on around you; however, as you moved towards the edge things became much more difficult to control, and at the very edge you were likely to be thrown off completely. Likewise, you know where you are with beer, but wander off into the chaotic world of Jaegerbombs and the world becomes a frightening and uncertain place.

W.B. Yeats helps us to visualize a world where all of the conventional beliefs are threatened. The aftermath of World War One has left a world unrecognisable to that which went before. Instead of steady progress, there is impending anarchy. It is *'mere anarchy'* in the sense that it is anarchy alone, and nothing else (as opposed to a light dusting or smidgen of anarchy). Such upheaval threatens to overwhelm everything and create a world of blood; a world where innocence is lost forever.

During the same period, Darwinism was undermining the core of Christian values; this, together with the aftermath of war, created a chaos in which *'The best lack all conviction, while the worst...Are full of passionate intensity.'* Intelligent people did not know what to believe anymore, while the frightened and gullible turned to religion or cults.

It is difficult to understand how beliefs in bizarre superstitions and interventionist Gods can exist despite such overwhelming evidence to the contrary; yet still they thrive. Any cursory search for 'meaning' on the internet will throw up websites of religious groups talking about the Exultation: a time when Christ will return, take his believers into everlasting bliss, and presumably everyone will indulge in a spot of exulting. Belief in the Exultation and the Apocalypse belong to the fringes of fundamentalist Christian belief, at least in the UK, but in countries like the USA they are growing. Strict adherence to such ideologies, like Communism in Russia in the 1990s, the flaming sword of ISIS in the Middle East, and Star Trek Fan fundamentalism, helps people to make sense of the world and relieves them of the cerebral exertion of having to work out the answers for themselves.

Stanza 2 (Part 1)

Surely some revelation is at hand;...Surely the Second Coming is at hand....The Second Coming! Hardly are those words out...When a vast image out of Spiritus Mundi...Troubles my sight: somewhere in sands of the desert...A shape with lion body and the head of a man,...A gaze blank and pitiless as the sun,...Is moving its slow thighs, while all about it...Reel shadows of the indignant desert birds.

It could have been the monkey gland talking, but Yeats believed that history occurred in cycles of two thousand years and that such a cycle began with the birth of Christ. This belief is reflected in the second stanza; in order to make sense of what is happening, people turn to religion. The signs point to the second coming, surely the new Messiah must come now; salvation is at hand and order will be restored.

The second coming of Christ is prophesied in the Bible, in the Book of Revelation, and throughout the ages people have speculated as to when the revelation of the new Messiah would occur and what it would mean. Such speculations have spawned numerous religious cults that profess to know the exact date of the second coming and what their followers should do in order to prepare for it (best type of crash helmet to wear, etc.). Religious movements cherry-pick passages from the Bible and other sources to confirm their faith in the coming event.

Not surprisingly, these cults tend to flourish at significant dates when religious leaders scrabble to capitalise upon irrational fears. At the end of the twentieth century, many religious groups formed and waited for the second coming or the end of the world. The end of the last millennium saw like-minded, small-minded, hand-wringing, head-bangers and tea-leaf readers predicting the coming of great change in the world. At the end of 1999, followers of New Age mysticism, and evangelical Christians alike, waited eagerly for the great event that would bring meaning or the end to the world...but nothing happened (which was nice). Things went on as usual, and predictions that the Millennium Bug would tamper with our toaster settings and send planes hurtling out of the skies, went unfulfilled. Well, most predictions went unfulfilled.

Even the most short-sighted of people could have predicted that Prince would make a brief 'second coming' of his own, what with everybody 'Partying like it was 1999'. Prince did not foresee the end of the world; he saw a good business opportunity. As did those bastards at Microsoft, who convinced us that we would lose all our music and saved games of *Command and Conquer* (along with other sensitive material), and cashed in by offering to four-horsemen-of-the-apocalypse-proof our PCs.

Just because the world hasn't ended yet, doesn't mean that it won't. In fact, it most certainly will. Hopefully the end will not come for a very long time, but we should never underestimate mankind's capacity to do something silly, like orchestrate its own Apocalypse. W.B Yeats's vision of the second coming has more to do with the destruction than the restoration of Christian values. From a world spun out of control, a desert waste of final destruction and spiritual emptiness, a new shape begins to stir and it will not bring comfort.

The Sphinx, a monster *'with lion body and the head of a man'* slowly stirs into life and is on the move. The animal body and human head of the Sphinx represent the opposite of the human body and animal head of the falconer and falcon; and unlike the falcon and falconer (congregations and their leadership), the Sphinx is not out of control. It is alive and moving towards us!

Stanza 2 (Part 2)

The darkness drops again; but now I know...That twenty centuries of stony sleep...Were vexed to nightmare by a rocking cradle,....And what rough beast, its hour come round at last,... Slouches towards Bethlehem to be born?

The vision of the Sphinx disappears, but it has revealed something important to the poet: twenty centuries of Christianity have finally toppled into chaos. The homeless infant, gentle Jesus meek and mild, has lost control and a future of chaos awaits; a future ruled by the new Messiah: The Beast.

Written in 1919, this poem offers a warning that we would do well to heed today. In Iraq and Syria, Israel and Palestine, Nigeria and even the USA, the Beast of Fundamentalism moves slowly onward, enveloping everything in its hideous nightmare.

So, how does the Manly Man single-handedly avert the Apocalypse? Well, he starts by rooting out dogma in his own life and the lives of others. Dogma, religious or otherwise, is the unhappy synchronicity of complimentary needs. Some people like to be controlled, to be given a set of instructions about how they should live (as if they were a f@*king vacuum cleaner), while others are more than happy to do the controlling. In general, the leaders who want to be in charge are below average in height, have 'serious' moustaches and are a single consonant away from being the complete cults that they represent.[32]

The Manly Man's penchant for dogma is restricted to repeatedly lifting heavy things off the ground and then setting them back down again in the belief that it will make them a better person. The only time that we get down on our knees is to work our triceps in the gym. The only time we summon belief from another world, is to force out one more rep. Lynx body spray is the incense with which we cover up the smell of our sweaty congregation whose cries of jubilation fill the air:

"Can I get a hallelujah?"…"Can I get one last rep?" "Hell-yeah!"

There is nothing more meditative than trying to put your mind outside your body when you decide to run that extra mile. Yet the Manly Man will never relinquish his manliness to self-obsession or the dogma of the body cult. He appreciates a good work out, but has no time for the tittle-tattle of the boring body worshippers who genuflex their biceps on the way out of the gym.

---

[32] Fear has always been good for business and these leaders use it to recruit followers who are searching for some form of certainty in an increasingly confused world. For some of these followers, the content of the religion is less important than their position within it. In the lower echelons, it is an exclusive club where one is accepted; higher up, opportunities exist for the ambitious, sanctimonious, and enterprising. People have always been prepared to cook the Good Book for a little free love, tax-free donations, and access to small boys.

It may not be easy in the face of pressure from peers and society, but the Manly Man writes his own instructions for living a worthy life; he has the discipline to develop good habits and the patience to pursue his dreams. The Manly Man has a mind open enough to accept other points of view, learn from the best of them, and update his view of the world accordingly; he engages in life's contradictive cornucopia of beliefs and activities. The gym is his Cathedral, the pub as his Confessional, and the Terminator is his Second Coming "I'll be back!"

Manlifesto: The Manly Man does not let others impose their dogma upon him; instead, he constructs his own manly set of values to which he devotes himself (without turning into a complete cult).

Part 3. Action Man: New model comes complete with cock and balls

Send No Money

Philip Larkin

In the days before supermarkets invited us all to BOGOF, "Send no money!" offers were used by advertisers to lure customers into trying a product they didn't need. "Send no money" was a real 'coin-teaser'; a sexy little phrase that would slip on its slinkiest black dress, slap on its reddest lipstick, and beckon the weak-willed with its index finger into the land of 'try before you buy'. The tactic worked because people couldn't be bothered to send the offending article back, not because the product improved the quality of people's lives immeasurably and they wondered how they had survived all those years without a *Soda Stream*.

If you were taking this poem for a test drive before buying it, you would be forgiven for sending it back to the poetry dealer. It doesn't even rhyme properly. This is shoddy workmanship: a half-finished, half-arsed attempt in serious need of the love of a good poetry mechanic, "Ah! Mate, there's your problem, suspension of disbelief is shot to hell and your iambic pentameter needs realigned in the final stanza." Or perhaps there is method in the slap-dashery, for the second part of each verse, or stanza (if we're being swanky), *does* rhyme. It could be that the first half of each stanza is a half-hearted affair that mirrors the lacklustre life led by the poem's protagonist.

In this poem, Philip Larkin reminds us that life is short. He offers a warning against misspent youth (or misspent middle age for that matter); a warning not heeded by the poem's protagonist: one of those dry-souled arseholes who leave life to the rest of us adventurers. Manly Men, gird your loins, buckle your swash and read on!

Send No Money

Standing under the fobbed
Impendent belly of Time
Tell me the truth, I said,
Teach me the way things go.
All the other lads there
Were itching to have a bash,
But I thought wanting unfair:
It and finding out clash.

So he patted my head, booming Boy,
There's no green in your eye:
Sit here and watch the hail
Of occurrence clobber life out
To a shape no one sees -
Dare you look at that straight?
Oh thank you, I said, Oh yes please,
And sat down to wait.

Half life is over now,
And I meet full face on dark mornings
The bestial visor, bent in
By the blows of what happened to happen.
What does it prove? Sod all.
In this way I spent youth,
Tracing the trite untransferable
Truss-advertisement, truth.

Stanza 1

Standing under the fobbed…Impendent belly of Time…Tell me the truth, I said,…Teach me the way things go…All the other lads there…Were itching to have a bash,…But I thought wanting unfair…It and finding out clash.

The language of this poem is conversational and informal. It could be the confessional of a sad-eyed, bar fly telling us a story about the time he met…well, Time. The poet personifies "Time" by bringing it to life with a capital T. Poets often whip out the magic anthropomorphic capital when they want to abracadabra something into human form (e.g. Death, Love and Lady Luck). The idea is that if something as powerful and mysterious as Time, or Death, can be seen in human form, it may make it easier for us to understand and come to terms with it. If Lady Luck is depicted as an attractive girl who can't make up her mind, it may help us to understand and accept the randomness of luck, especially when she screws us over. In any case, many men would find it preferable to be screwed over by Lady Luck than by Mr T (Time): a big bad ass mo'fo' with gold teeth.

So, in this poem, Time is a figure imagined by the poet. Mr T even has some bling, a watch on a chain; most appropriate! He also has a big overhanging belly and the word *'impending'* implies that something is about to happen. (Perhaps he is about to burst out of a shed with the rest of the *A-Team* in a tank they cobbled together from an old pram, a leaf blower and a piece of drain pipe sellotaped to a broom handle).

The first stanza paints Time as a big friendly 'brother from another mother,' full of good advice, and that is exactly what the young lad in the poem asks for. What would you ask Time about if you had the chance? The young man in the poem wants to know the truth about his future, so that he can be prepared for whatever life has in store; only Time knows the answer and only Time will tell.

Our young protagonist watches as everyone around him, '*all of the other lads*', are busy doing or wanting to do all sorts of interesting things, particularly with their penis. The one big experience that most young lads look forward to is, of course, getting some sexy time. In the poet's own eloquent words, they are all '*itching to have a bash*'. All except our young hero. The last line of the first verse, '*But I thought wanting unfair: It and finding out clash*', suggests that the young man thinks he is smarter than his mates.

Despite his inexperience, the young man already suspects that the reality of an experience is never as good as the anticipation of it. He senses that once the itch is scratched and satisfaction is achieved, he will be left feeling unfulfilled. He is far too clever for that and will forgo the superficial pleasures of the moment. He's above drinking, womanising, and beeping the horn at someone and then waving the other way.

Smugly, the young man watches and laughs at the efforts of others; their failure is his victory and vindication for not trying. He hangs around to watch the other lads waste their time, unaware that wasting time is exactly what *they* are not doing (and *he* is)!

Stanza 2

So he patted my head, booming Boy,…There's no green in your eye:…Sit here and watch the hail…Of occurrence clobber life out…To a shape no one sees -…Dare you look at that straight?…Oh thank you, I said, Oh yes please,…And sat down to wait.

With a paternal pat on the head and a compliment, Time's advice is to wait and see. The randomness of events will shape a person's experience into a pattern that can only be seen when it ends. Time will pass, events will occur, and the shape of each life will be formed. Time dares him to watch the randomness unfold. A dare implies danger but also a reward. A task is undertaken, difficulties are overcome and our hero emerges an older and a wiser man.[33] In the poem, our 'hero' rises to Time's challenge, but his reply is less than heroic.

'Oh thank you, I said, Oh yes please, And sat down to wait'.

The humour is evident. Here is our hero, a daring adventurer, with the truth about to be revealed to him at any moment! And what is he doing? Nothing. This is the story of a coward rather than a participant; the guy who suggests swimming in the sea on a winter's day, and then pretends to have forgotten his trunks.[34]

All around the young man, life twirls and spins; people are having a bash while he waits. Time passes…the young man's future approaches at the speed of one second per second and it too passes. Time checks his watch and smiles down on him. The man who patronises his mates, is in turn patronized by Time. Time is no man's friend. Time is happy to sit back and gobble up your seconds. Whether you like it or not, Time is always up to its old trick of making things happen.

Stanza 3

Half life is over now,….And I meet full face on dark mornings…The bestial

---

[33] He may even earn some manly scars and a flaxen-haired maiden or two for his trouble.

[34] Not that he would have anything to fill them with.

visor, bent in...By the blows of what happened to happen...What does it prove? Sod all...In this way I spent youth,...Tracing the trite untransferable...Truss-advertisement, truth.

The final stanza moves from a time of youthful hope and innocence to the present, a time when the truth has become evident and the experience of time passing is revealed every day in the mirror. In the previous stanza, Time dared the young man to look at the result of his decisions full in the face. Now our hero gets his reward. Now his mornings are dark, and the meaningless hail of events that have made up his life have left their mark on the unappealing, *'bestial visor'* of the animal-like face that stares back at him. Experience has been painful; it has delivered blows, bent and aged him.

But surely experience makes us better people? Does time not make us wiser and stronger? The wisdom of age is the product of time... and so on. Our hero has waited and waited, and Time has clobbered out the pattern of his life. He has been fashioned into one of those sad elements of the world that nobody would notice had they not been fashioned at all, like word-search puzzles or Jeremy Kyle/Paris Hilton. It is a pattern that for all the young man's foresight he was unable to predict. Only now, does he realize the bleak *'untransferable'* truth that stares out at him every morning: time will pass anyway, whether we pay attention to it or not. And what does having such knowledge mean? *"What does it prove? Sod all,"* I'm afraid. This knowledge does not give us any more control or influence over the passing of time...but it should give us a good kick up the arse!

This is a poem of misspent youth. However, it is the youth of our narrator that has been frittered away, rather than that of his mates who made the most of their time having a bash! Like money thrown down the drain, the young man has spent his time on nothing of value. 'Send no money!' The young man is a victim of misadvertising and has been sold a rubbish life. All the promise of his youth has ended, beaten down beneath the endless tread of time. Time has passed, and unfortunately there is nothing that can be done about it. This is not *Back to the Future* and the young man is not *Doctor Who*. He is Mr Nobody. Time is a con man who has sold him a bum deal.

But such a fate is not for the Manly Man who knows his poetry. The Manly Man knows that those who detach themselves from life, fearful of the potential pain arising from a 3-day bender in Poland, or heartbreak at the hands of a stunner, will never know the satisfaction of drunken bonhomie, or the happy surprise when, on the 40th attempt, the princess kisses the frog. Poetry teaches us how to pull the woollen jumper over the head of Time, give it a kick in the nuts, and steal our seconds back.[35]

Manlifesto: The Manly Man knows that life is short and that the only thing worse than fear of death is fear of life: not living life to the full for fear of failure and rejection. The Manly Man would rather Jaegerbomb into the pool of life and accept the collateral damage, than be a bottle of alcohol-free beer left on the shelf.

---

[35] This poem may be a little preachy, but some sermons are worth listening too, and it is only in the temple of poetry that the priest gives a lesson about how his flock should all go out on the rip and shag one another:

"Forgive me father for I have sinned. I left a pint half-finished at the bar last night, did not laugh at my mate's overly-tight shirt and turned down a quick snog at the taxi rank."

"Don't worry my son. That will be 6 bloody Marys, 7 Guinness, and a wee wank. Don't let it happen again!"

Any God worth believing in wants you to enjoy yourself and poetry can help you justify it!

The Owl

Edward Thomas

There is nothing quite as satisfying to the sensibilities of the Manly Man as rising to a seemingly masochistic challenge, where he tests his body and mind against Nature or his fellow man, emerging from the battle, a battered, but bettered, person. Whether it be a mountain conquered, a marathon ran, or a game of rugby played on a frozen pitch, we have all enjoyed that happy afterglow of physical exertion, when our aching bodies are rewarded with a well-earned rest and a few sneaky pints…maybe even a foam bath.[36] However, this poem by Teddy Thomas warns us not to take ourselves nor our victories too seriously, and contrasts our physical achievements and 'hardships' with those of people who know about real heroism and suffering.

This poem reminds us that while dominating a Tough Mudder obstacle course or completing an Ironman Triathlon endurance race, is very impressive, it is also a bit silly in the grand scheme of things. There are parts of the world where old women and soldiers are covering the same distances on empty stomachs, under fire from a hostile enemy; places where the contestants must negotiate landmines rather than fiendishly arranged tractor tyres, and the prize is keeping your teeth rather than a free t-shirt. For a lesson in the modesty of the Manly Man, read on.

---

36 Which can still be manly provided you replace herbal bath salts with Mr Matey and any rubber ducks with bottles of whiskey.

The Owl

DOWNHILL *I came, hungry, and yet not starved,*
Cold, yet had heat within me that was proof
Against the north wind; tired, yet so that rest
Had seemed the sweetest thing under a roof.

Then at the inn I had food, fire, and rest,
Knowing how hungry, cold, and tired was I.
All of the night was quite barred out except
An owl's cry, a most melancholy cry.

Shaken out long and clear upon the hill
No merry note, nor cause of merriment,
But one telling me plain what I escaped
And others could not, that night, as in I went.

And salted was my food, and my repose,
Salted and sobered too, by the bird's voice
Speaking for all who lay under the stars,
Soldiers and poor, unable to rejoice.

Stanza 1

DOWNHILL *I came, hungry, and yet not starved,…Cold, yet had heat within me that was proof,…Against the north wind; tired, yet so that rest,…Had seemed the sweetest thing under a roof*

This poem has four stanzas, with four lines in each. The first stanza is one long sentence, which reflects the poet's long trudge '*downhill*', as he makes his way home after a long hike in the mountains. The poet is hungry and cold; he has pushed himself to the point of exhaustion, but is comforted by the knowledge

74

that his self-imposed suffering will soon be over. Exposure to the brutal elements and hunger makes the poet feel alive. Perversely, these hardships feel quite pleasant when the promise of rest and comfort are close at hand. Already the poet is eagerly anticipating a well-deserved meal and very probably looking forward to having a massive dump that he has been holding in for the last half an hour.

We have all had similar feelings and fantasies as we make our way back home from a particularly hard outdoor training session or weekend camping in the wilderness. As we make our way back to civilization, we can already see ourselves sitting in a high-backed leather chair by the fire, swirling a glass of fine Spanish brandy in our hand; the faint smell of sea salt and fish guts still in our nostrils; somewhere in the background pots rattle together as our catch is prepared by a beautiful milkmaid who is driven into a sexual frenzy by our all-round, hunter-gathering Manly-Manfulness. Failing that, a cup of tea and a chocolate Hobnob would do nicely.

Stanza 2

Then at the inn I had food, fire, and rest,… Knowing how hungry, cold, and tired was I….All of the night was quite barred out except,…An owl's cry, a most melancholy cry.

In stanza two the poet makes it back to the inn and all his expectations and physical needs are met: he has food for his hunger, a fire to drive away the cold, a place to relax and a never-ending roll of luxury, quilted toilet paper.[37] The pleasure of

---

[37] As well as that special peace of mind when you can take a shit without worrying about being eaten by a bear.

fulfilled anticipation shuts out all of the hardships of the cold, dark night. As the poet wallows in a hot bath of smug self-satisfaction, he relives the adventure in his mind's eye, embellishing it with feats of bravado to create a tale of heroism in which he is a knight in shining armour. [38]

The poet is just beginning to savour his comfort and heroic deeds, when an *'owl's cry'* screeches through his warm, fuzzy feeling of self-satisfaction and disturbs his rest. The long, sad cry of the owl reminds the poet of those left outside in the cold and dark through no fault of their own. When we flirt with danger and hardship, our thoughts, like those of the poet, turn to those less fortunate. [39] The poet slowly recognizes how lucky he is to be able to choose hardship and challenges rather than have them thrust upon him.

Stanza 3

Shaken out long and clear upon the hill,... No merry note, nor cause of merriment,...But one telling me plain what I escaped,...And others could not, that night, as in I went.

---

[38] Like fat business men adventuring *'first-class'*, who waddle up Kilimanjaro or Machu Picchu convinced that they are brave explorers, even though they have their food, tents and toiletries carried for them by guides as if they were fairy-tale princesses. As they walk, they are already concocting tales of daring-do to regale family and friends on their return. Meanwhile, the guides climb under conditions of necessity and for reasons far more noble than wealthy tourists; the only self-congratulation they indulge in is reserved for ripping-off the flaccid-buttocked businessmen.

[39] The only way that most of us will ever experience proper, involuntary hardship is by accident. Sometimes a lack of foresight, complacency, or a few too many beers can force us into uncomfortable situations, such as: being caught out in the rain whilst running with no Vaseline on your nipples; walking in the wrong type of socks; sleeping in the summer tent that would "do rightly" and was "warmer than it looked," until it is pitched atop a snow-capped peak and you're lying beneath its icicle covered roof praying for morning to come and for the toe fairy to spare your little piggies.

76

The melancholy cry of an owl is unlike that of any other bird. Its long, sad cry seems to give voice to all the souls who are unable to find peace and comfort; to all the displaced and deprived people for whom rest is not an option, let alone the chance to relax in the luxury of an inn. It is a call that shatters schadenfreude, that cheerful knowledge that while your mates are still bracing the wind and the cold, you have made it back to the hotel and into the shower. This guilty pleasure normally makes the water even warmer and adds an extra layer of fuzz to your dressing gown, but it can only be truly enjoyed if you know that your friends will be OK; a Manly Man never leaves a man (Manly or otherwise) behind.

There is something profound and sobering about the call of the owl that pierces the poet's self-satisfaction and preoccupation with his own well-being. Just like the desperate and displaced, the owl is still outside in the cold darkness. The poet's thoughts turn away from his own sense of well-being to those for whom hunger, cold and exhaustion are a real threat. He begins to suspect that all of his macho pastimes are a little bit silly, and that there are better things that he could be doing with his time and energy.[40]

Stanza 4

And salted was my food, and my repose,....Salted and sobered too, by the bird's voice,.... Speaking for all who lay under the stars,... Soldiers and poor, unable to rejoice.

The poet's experience is transformed by '*the bird's voice*'. A sharp,

---

[40] This maudlin turn of thought could be explained by the fact that the poet is too tired to make important decisions and has ordered gin instead of whiskey.

harshness has invaded the sweet pleasures of food and repose. The salt tang brings out the true flavour of food and brings a bitter realism to the situation; it reminds him of the products of suffering, blood, sweat and tears, which are also salty. The bitter taste of his food and the sobering cry of the owl,[41] *'speaking for all who lay under the stars'*, focuses the poet's thoughts on the suffering of all those without a roof over their head.

The poet's sympathy turns to *'soldiers'* who have no choice, but to brave the battlefield, and the *'poor'* who must fight hunger and poverty in order to survive and support their family; people for whom suffering is a reality rather than a game. Their challenges and ordeals offer little opportunity for self-satisfaction beyond that of self-preservation, with the opportunity to struggle again the next day their only reward. The poet knows that to rejoice in his own comfort would be like rubbing salt into the wounds of the soldiers and the poor still suffering in the cold night.

It is in our nature to challenge ourselves, to heighten the intensity of life's pleasures through delayed gratification and the tackling of adversity. Every Manly Man is Don Quixote, fighting invisible foes, swashbuckling their way through each day, like little boys playing at pirates hunting for treasure. However, the Manly Man acknowledges the joy and limitations of adventuring for the sake of adventuring, and appreciates that there may be a better way for him to use his time and energy. Where possible, he trains with others in order to motivate and support them, and uses challenges as an excuse to raise money and awareness for charities. He uses

---

[41] The call of the owl has always been associated with the night and death…as well as boobies and classy American restaurants (Hooters).

his 'achievements' to motivate and inspire others, rather than impress them…but sometimes he just has to climb a mountain simply because it's there (and looked at him the wrong way).[42]

The Manly Man also understands that most of the hardships he has to endure are voluntary, and his glories are trivial compared to those of the real champions of adversity: the soldiers and destitute who have no choice but to grit their teeth and face down the shit-storm that Life throws at them. However, rather than wallow in his own glory or the misery of others, the Manly Man raises a glass to his own luck and the plight of others, before it all becomes too sobering…*'and salted was his Tequila slammer'.*

Manlifesto: The Manly Man takes satisfaction from training hard and rising to a challenge; however, he never takes himself or his achievements too seriously and never confuses a half-marathon finisher's medal with the St George's Cross.

---

[42] There is something superior, and uppity, in the way a mountain carries itself; an arrogance that comes from the knowledge that it is so much more permanent than we are. It is up to the Manly Man to wipe that smug look from off its rock face.

When I Have Fears that I May Cease to Be

John Keats

It is clear from the title of this poem that it deals with the serious business of death. Even though death is not something that we want to dwell upon, it is something that all Manly Men, even Jean Claude van Damme, must come face to face with. We all deal with our own mortality in different ways; while pretend men puff out their chests and act as though they laugh in the face of Death, the Manly Man has a bit more respect, and is sure to put on his crash helmet (and maybe some knee pads) before he starts laughing.[43]

Poets often treat death with a mawkish, gurning sentimentality, but not John Keats, he wrote poetry with honesty (and with his crash helmet on).[44] In this poem, Keats explains that he is not afraid of death, rather he is afraid of a life unfulfilled. He shares his fears and doubts about whether he has the time or ability to fulfil his dream of becoming a great poet. This poem reassures us that even the most Manly of Men doubt themselves and reminds us that it is important to remain true to our dreams.[45]

---

[43] The Manly Man wears a helmet when base-jumping off a cliff in a flying squirrel suit in the hope that this small courtesy will persuade Death to spare him should things go wrong...not because he believes that the helmet has any real protective properties.

[44] Unfortunately for Keats, a crash helmet offers little protection against *Tuberculosis*, which he died from at the age of 25. This poem is often seen, mistakenly, as Keats' foreboding sense of what was going to happen to him; a sort of morbid dwelling on his own death. However, Keats was no Mystic Meg; if he had of been able to foresee the future, he probably would have shared less opium pipes with badgers.

[45]Disclaimer: Being true to a dream, doesn't necessarily mean that it will come true. If you are a 37-year old chain-smoker who still dreams of playing for Manchester United,

Keats urges us to live our lives with courage and to never forget that the real tragedy is not death, but an unfulfilled life.

When I Have Fears that I May Cease to Be

When I have fears that I may cease to be
Before my pen has glean'd my teeming brain,
Before high piled books, in charact'ry,
Hold like rich garners the full-ripen'd grain;
When I behold, upon the night's starr'd face,
Huge cloudy symbols of a high romance,
And feel that I may never live to trace
Their shadows, with the magic hand of chance;
And when I feel, fair creature of an hour!
That I shall never look upon thee more,
Never have relish in the faery power
Of unreflecting love;—then on the shore
Of the wide world I stand alone, and think,
Till Love and Fame to nothingness do sink.

This poem is a sonnet made up of fourteen lines and appears, on the face of things, to be a lesson in bad grammar.[46] The first line is one of the longest sentences, ever; the sort that your high-school teacher would have butchered and returned to you sliced and diced, a blood-red-spattered fragment of its former self.[47] Keats hated a full stop, but he really loved an apostrophe; there's

---

or if you dream of being a flying toaster, it's OK to doubt that dream...it might not come true; but anything else is possible.

[46] Your Manly memory no doubt remembers what a sonnet is from *'On First Looking In to Chapman's Homer'*. If not, get down and gives us 30 press-ups.

[47] Or corrected in red pen (it depends on how personally you take it when Mrs Smith destroys your essay entitled: 'Macbeth and the Dangers of Taking Careers Advice from a Panel of Witches (Without a GCSE between Them).'

a disproportionate amount of these floaty little fellows litter'd and scatter'd throughout the rest of the poem, elbowing 'e's out of the way as they go.[48] However, despite this poem's unusual structure and grammar, its message is clear: 'Life is short, so do what you can while you can.'

Lines 1-4

When I have fears that I may cease to be...Before my pen has glean'd my teeming brain,...Before high piled books, in charact'ry,...Hold like rich garners the full-ripen'd grain;

Many lazy writers and poets exploit the subject of death in a maudlin attempt to gain our sympathy or manipulate us into feeling sad.[49] Unlike the misery merchants who would play our heart-strings like a banjo, Keats uses death and his Manly fear of living a life that is unfulfilled to inspire us into making the most of what little time we have.

Keats is a dream-gleaner. Gleaners were women who went into the fields after harvest to gather up any fallen grains so that nothing went to waste. Their modern contemporaries, the 'Gin-Gleaners', can be seen down your local night-club, after hours.[50]

---

[48]Keats was not a fan of 'e's; he was old school and happy enough to stick to the opium thank you very much.

[49]Keats was above the cheap tricks used by writers of 'chic lit' and Disney cartoons; however, he would have been capable of a tear-jerker. Keats was smart enough to have written a poem about a sick baby, orphaned on Christmas Eve, when its parents were killed by an evil holocaust-denying property developer who burned down their ice-cream factory where they made free ice-cream for the poor out of recycled milk. Knowing Keats, that baby would have survived, setting things up nicely for the follow-up poem; a tale of the revenge: 'When you have fears that I shall make you cease to be!'

[50] These shadow-like creatures emerge from the darkness, the moment you hit the dance floor, to finish off the dregs of your pint, any blue WKD knocking about, and run their tongues blindly along the inside of shot glasses to mop up any droplets of Jaeger or Cointreau.

Like the gleaners, Keats does not want a single drop of his creativity to go to waste; he wants to harvest and collect every idea of his active imagination, to write everything down before he dies. The harvest of his life's work will be shelves piled high with the books that he has still yet to write.

At the age of 18, Keats decided to become one of the best poets ever; a rather ambitious aim for a science student who didn't know how to use a full stop.[51] Imagine the cheek of this young man to think he could mix it up with the illustrious figures of English poetry, such as Milton, Shakespeare and Wordsworth. Even still, Wordsworth, who was still alive at the time, would have been constantly looking over his shoulder, worrying that his place as the greatest living poet was under threat as Keats' writing gradually improved.[52]

Some of Keats' contemporaries mocked him, and his stepfather told him to get a proper job. Most likely the old dinosaur felt that if his stepson was going to pursue an effeminate career, it ought to at least pay the bills (like dressmaking or stripping). But Keats did not want to be a stripper; he wanted to be a poet. Therefore, he dedicated himself to the career of his dreams with the naive fervour of a youngster who decides they are going to play for Manchester United and lived, breathed, and presumably shat poetry in an attempt to make it happen. A good rhyming couplet was Keats' last minute winner, careful editing his lung-bursting run from box to box, and he was never afraid to go in for a 50-50 sliding tackle (studs showing) with a word that only

---

[51] If articles published in scientific journals are anything to go by, most science degrees include a module on 'Grammar Abuse'. In general, scientists are suspicious of good grammar, without suspecting that it might make their articles less impenetrable.

[52] Although, Wordsworth ought to have been more worried about Keats following him home, tying him to the bedposts, breaking his legs, and making him write a proper ending to 'The Prelude'. (Keats was Wordsworth's number 1 fan).

just about rhymed. All of that effort and training was vindicated as Keats managed to stay injury-free to become a good poet in his own lifetime, and a great one after his death.[53]

Lines 5-8

When I behold, upon the night's starr'd face,...Huge cloudy symbols of a high romance,....And feel that I may never live to trace...Their shadows, with the magic hand of chance;

Keats was also a dreamer. When he looks up at the night sky his imagination soars. His thoughts teem with the kinds of subjects he wants to write about; tales of Knights and High Romance, castles and elopements. He is consumed by the urgency of the task he has set himself but he is equally beset with doubts. For a moment, Keats doubts whether he has the time or talent to pin down his ideas, to trace the shifting shadows of his imagination, and capture it all with ink on paper. The first eight lines of this sonnet end with Keats doubting whether he is capable of producing the type of poetry he yearns to write.

Lines 9-14

And when I feel, fair creature of an hour!...That I shall never look upon thee more,...Never have relish in the faery power...Of unreflecting love;—then on the shore...Of the wide world I stand alone, and think,...Till Love and Fame to nothingness do sink.

---

[53] It is interesting to note that for all the abuse thrown at footballers for being vain, greedy and stupid, at least they have had the wisdom to choose a profession in which they are appreciated as they practice it. David Beckham was considered a great dead-ball specialist, without having to be dead. Such a happy fate is not shared by artists who, in general, only become famous and 'understood' after they die. On the other hand, nobody is going to look back at video tapes of Nobby Stiles or Robbie Savage and reinvent them as misunderstood geniuses who were before their time (and not complete hatchet men...with bad hair).

In the first eight lines of the poem, Keats expressed his doubts and daydreams, his imagination taking flight into the realms of make-believe. Now, towards the end of poem, his thoughts become less abstract and focus on the face of a beautiful girl.

The *'fair creature'* is the embodiment of Keats' imaginative creativity. Keats' love for her is *'unreflecting'* because it is unconditional and requires no second thoughts. The *'faery power'* he talks about is not that of wand-brandishing tooth burglars, but the power of the *'fair creature'* to inspire his imagination and help him become a great poet. She is the muse that inspires him and breathes life into his work.[54] Keats would be left inconsolable if such a love were taken away from him.

Keats doesn't know what he would do if this inspiration were ever to abandon him. He would be left like an empty husk, with nothing to show for a lifetime of work; alone in a strange world, where all his hopes of finding love and success would dwindle away to nothingness. Fortunately, Keats was born in the days before X-Box, cheap beer and the abundant paraphernalia we have nowadays to help us cope with, and actively encourage, a meaningless life.

Despite all the self-doubt and criticism from others, Keats kept his dream burning right until his death and became one of the greatest poets of all time. Keats died young but the harvest of his life sits on millions of bookshelves all over the world, including your own.[55]

---

[54] Artists often have these imaginary friends who follow them about, offering inspiration and words of encouragement when they most need them: a bit like Pete's Dragon, Calvin's stuffed tiger, Hobbes, or Jesus.

[55] Keats' greatness is reflected in what may be his finest achievement: three entries in *The Manly Book of Poems for Men*.

This poem is the expression of a young man's yearning to fulfil his life's ambitions. Just as Keats is haunted by empty bookshelves, the Manly Man is taunted by uncut grass, unbuilt sheds and unfinished projects. Even though we may doubt whether we can get all our doings done in this short life, we have a responsibility to try and complete the great works of which we are capable; whether it be a happy family, friends appreciated, a sexy lover satisfied, or a yard of ale downed.

The Manly Man uses self-criticism and doubt to make sure that his work is the best that it can be, rather than as an excuse not to try in the first place. Lesser men are seduced by Cowardice, which tarts itself up in the fancy frock of self-doubt to seduce us with excuses for not following a dream. But that's not for us! Like Keats, the Manly Man is more afraid of living an unfulfilled life, than death. We worry about not doing justice to our abilities and the abilities of others. Life is short, the least we can do is to have a few dreams, make plans in harmony with those dreams, and do our best to follow them. So, chloroform Time (Mr. T), put on your dinosaur suit, light up a cigar and love it when a plan comes together (and don't beat yourself up too much when it doesn't).

Manlifesto: The Manly Man blows a raspberry on the yellow belly of doubt, puts on his crash helmet and throws himself into the most death-defying act of all: a worthy life.

Whatever Happened

Philip Larkin

The title of this poem asks the question *'Whatever Happened?'* Although a more appropriate question could be 'Whatever happened to make Philip Larkin such a miserable bugger?' It could be the relentless passage of time, the uncertainty of memory and Life's indifference to the fate of Mankind and his trousers, which are the key themes of this poem.

Life has an irritating habit of making things happen to us, without running them by us first to see if it's OK. This poem reminds the Manly Man that although he may not be able to control all of the events that happen to him, he can control how he remembers them; as an event recedes into the past, we can decide how much significance it has and how it will affect our present. This poem can help the Manly Man come to terms with that last-minute penalty miss, and maybe even justify *'Whatever Happened'* with that Thai Lady Boy in Bangkok as just one of those things…

Whatever Happened?

At once whatever happened starts receding.
Panting, and back on board, we line the rail
With trousers ripped, light wallets, and lips bleeding.

Yes, gone, thank God! Remembering each detail
We toss for half the night, but find next day

All's kodak-distant. Easily, then (though pale),

'Perspective brings significance,' we say,
Unhooding our photometers, and, snap!
What can't be printed can be thrown away.

Later, it's just a latitude: the map
Points out how unavoidable it was:
'Such coastal bedding always means mishap.'

Curses? The dark? Struggling? Where's the source
Of these yarns now (except in nightmares, of course)?

Stanza 1

At once whatever happened starts receding....Panting, and back on board, we
line the rail...With trousers ripped, light wallets, and lips bleeding.

The poem begins with an event that has just finished: a brush with the law, a near miss at the traffic lights, or a particularly enthusiastic and expensive spot of romancing that has left '*...trousers ripped, light wallets, and lips bleeding*'. Whatever it was, the moment has now sailed from the present into the past, like the ship of missed opportunities in *Send No Money*, another poem by Larkin in *The Manly Book of Poems for Men*. We are with the poet as the event recedes into the past at the rate of one second per second.

The incident has momentarily disrupted the monotony of our ordinary lives with a little excitement. We have grappled with '*whatever happened*' and come away bearing the scars and the stories. Like heroes in a cheap novel or comic book, we have managed, at the last moment, to get '*back on board*' our normal, non-eventful lives and are grateful to grip the rail of what we think of as reality once more.

Stanza 2

Yes, gone, thank God! Remembering each detail…We toss for half the night, but find next day…All's Kodak-distant. Easily, then (though pale),…

'Yes, gone, thank God!' The poet's sense of relief is clear. Now that self-preservation has been secured, the poet's thoughts turn to how we process and deal with events after they have happened; how we blame ourselves for what was done or not done at the time, and *'toss for half the night'* in bed with pangs of guilt and anguish. The marks left on us by the event are still raw on our skin and in our emotions. In the darkness, we relive the event over and over in our head, hoping to make sense of it through a frenzy of over analysis.

Fortunately, most things look better in the morning. The next day we can stand back from the event and view it like we would a photograph. *'All's Kodak-distant'*. The complicated tangle that led to *'trousers ripped'*, *'light wallets'*, and *'lips bleeding'* is frozen in time and simplified into one fixed image that we can make sense of. The whole episode is screened by our brains and conveniently reduced to a few simple components in harmony with how we view the world. We are left with a single snapshot that we understand and everything else is ditched overboard and forgotten.

The Photoshopping of events by our memories is just one way that our brains protect us from some harsh realities. It is far better to have the subjective memory of being a drunken charmer, than hard video footage of you tottering around a taxi depot, with a kebab on your head, trying to chat up a Skoda Superb.

Stanza 3

'Perspective brings significance,' we say,…Unhooding our photometers, and, snap!…What can't be printed can be thrown away.

Fortunately, *'perspective brings significance'*, and it allows us to attach our own meaning to the event before we file it away as a new photograph in our collection of memories. '*Snap!*' We simplify the event and choose which bits to keep and which to discard, so what we remember is what we choose to remember. Our choice is selective and so the event becomes a story that is recreated every time it is told. We become the dashing hero in a drama of our own creation, a drama that we have reduced to the *Snap! Wham! Pow!* of comic-book simplicity. The word comic is appropriate because of the humorous exaggeration of the event and the school-boy absurdity of the hero clinging to the rail like Indiana Jones.

Stanza 4

Later, it's just a latitude: the map…Points out how unavoidable it was:…'Such coastal bedding always means mishap.'

As we sail onward through time, our distance from the event increases, and we are affected less and less by it. We can look back at the route we took, charting the course of our lives through key events, and take comfort ourselves with *'how unavoidable it was.'*

We did our best to navigate treacherous waters, but running aground now and again was to be expected.

Every now and then, just when you think that all is ship-shape, the tides turn, the wind kicks up and you are momentarily cast adrift, but that's the price of adventure. It is better to be a shipwrecked galleon, weighed-down on the seabed with treasure, than a boat that never left the shore.

Life has no map, no set course for us to follow. Even if it did, all maps are unreliable at best and lying toe-rags at worst. They suggest a certain effortlessness to a journey, a security and unsubstantiated confidence that the path will inevitably lead to its destination, which makes it all the more galling and surprising when everything goes to shit. Maps fail to show us where we will get blisters on our feet, be blasted by a thunderstorm, or ambushed by bandits. If a plan is just a list of things that can go wrong, then a map is a nice, easy to understand, infographic of the shit storm.

However, it's this unpredictability that makes maps so compelling, that makes us want trace our fingers along its lines and daydream about where we might go and the accidental adventures we would have: a last-minute parachute jump on holiday, a career change sparked by sending a drunken email or even a bit of 'coastal bedding', which is presumably a poetic euphemism for sexy time in the sand dunes.

Last 2 lines

Curses? The dark? Struggling? Where's the source...Of these yarns now (except in nightmares, of course)?

The final two lines of the poem *Batman* back to the clichéd language of a comic book. *'Curses?', Yikes, Kapow!* Our 'hero' has overcome and survived the event, which has now become a *'yarn'* to be retold in the bar. Lesser men often spout tall tales of glory about how brave they were and how much she loved it, when the truth is they were terrified and she most definitely didn't.

However, every now and then, the stark truth of the events bubble to the surface in recurring *'nightmares'* that have power to jolt us awake in the dark.[56]

Day after day, time slips away in a flurry of events. Moments flash by, excitement fades and then we are on to the next thrill, the next episode, another distraction. Moment by moment we are subconsciously collecting memories, which we then classify and file away, without giving them a second thought. The problem is that memories don't appreciate being suppressed, misrepresented and ignored. Left unchecked, this resentment festers and simmers, until it boils over into a full blown revolution of regret that storms the ramparts when you're at your most vulnerable.

But the Manly Man is ready for such an attack because he has read a bit of Phillip Larkin. The Manly Man knows that it is important to reflect on memories, accept *'whatever happened'* and learn from the experience. He focuses on the positive, takes heart from his successes, and refuses to dwell on his mistakes. If memories are just unreliable stories that we tell ourselves, they may as well be positive! So stock up on good memories, shove two fingers into the face of regret, and say "Your mother was a

---

[56] Normally at around 0400 am after eating a late-night curry or a few too many Dairylea triangles.

hamster, and your father smells of elderberries, "in your best French accent.

Manlifesto: The Manly Man doesn't do misery memories. He learns from his mistakes and takes heart from his successes; he knows that memory is essentially a story and choses to re-read *The Bourne Identity* rather than *Goodbye Mog.*[57]

---

[57] Spoiler Alert: *Goodbye Mog* is the saddest *Meg and Mog* book ever, and made it into the *Daily Telegraph* newspaper's top 15 most depressing books of all time (Mog the Cat dies!).

Part 4. Love and Loss: Lessons in love from the Chat-Up Merchant of Venice and friends

Sonnet 18: Shall I Compare Thee to a Summer's Day?

William Shakespeare

Sonnet 18 is a love poem written by everybody's favourite frilly-collared fellow, William Shakespeare. As you now know, a sonnet is a poem comprised of fourteen lines: the first eight lines generally set up an argument or theme, after which, the final six lines either explain the argument further or turn it on its head in an exercise of intellectual back-trackery. For example, a Jeremy ClarkSonnet kicks off with eight lines of ill-judged commentary about the poor quality of cars made by half-witted foreigners who (Clarkson believes) wear shoes made out of coconuts, followed by six lines of 'oops-a-daisiery', where Clarkson attempts to make his casual racism more palatable with a 'positive' comment about the same demographic; something along the lines of their expertise in making a jolly good Tikka Masala or carrying stuff up mountains for rich tourists.

While a ClarkSonnet is essentially a lesson in being a pillock, Shakespeare's *Sonnet 18* is a lesson in love, immortality and the art of seduction. In this poem, Shakespeare teaches the Manly Man how to develop a killer compliment and elevate his chat-up lines to a level beyond 'Was your daddy a leprechaun?'[58]

Sonnet 18: Shall I Compare Thee to a Summer's Day?

Shall I compare thee to a summer's day?

---

[58] 'Because *Irish* you were naked!'

Thou art more lovely and more temperate:
Rough winds do shake the darling buds of May,
And summer's lease hath all too short a date:
Sometime too hot the eye of heaven shines,
And often is his gold complexion dimm'd;
And every fair from fair sometime declines,
By chance, or nature's changing course, untrimm'd;
But thy eternal summer shall not fade
Nor lose possession of that fair thou ow'st;
Nor shall Death brag thou wander'st in his shade,
When in eternal lines to time thou grow'st;
So long as men can breathe or eyes can see,
So long lives this, and this gives life to thee.

Lines 1-4

Shall I compare thee to a summer's day?...Thou art more lovely and more temperate:...Rough winds do shake the darling buds of May,...And summer's lease hath all too short a date:

Shakespeare's first lesson in love and seduction is that you should stick to inanimate objects when making any flattering comparisons. Shakespeare's genius lies not so much in comparing his loved one to a summer's day, as not comparing her to another female. Earnestly asking the object of your desire, 'Shall I compare thee to Doris Day?' (or Scarlett Johansson) may result in your groin receiving attention that is less friendly (and more *kicky*) than intended. A good simile has the power to flatter and seduce, but pick your comparisons with care; while the sun is a fairly safe bet, comparing your lover to the village bicycle is misinterpreted in some cultures.[59] This type of flattery is good chat and has been used throughout history from, 'My love is like a red, red rose,' to the immortal word-smithery of Robert Kelly, 'I'm feelin' you, the way you do the things you do, reminds me of my Lexus Coupe. Please let me put my key in your ignition.' However, the real key is to compare the beauty of your lover to something so harmless that not even the most possessive of lovers could accuse you of wanting to have sex with it.[60]

As far as compliments go, '*a summer's day*' would be a good place to start for mere mortals, but not for the chat-up Merchant of Venice. Shakespeare knows that such a comparison is clichéd and predictable, so he gets up inside his lover's mind with some clever-cloggery. You see, sometimes the sun is not always the benevolent extrovert that whores itself out all over the Mediterranean. In England, the climate is unpredictable and sunny days are few and far between;[61] the sun is an object of rare beauty and appreciated all the more when it makes an appearance. Consequently, being compared to sunshine on '*a summer's day*' is a compliment. Shakespeare is saying that the object of his affections is lovelier and more steadfast than the summer which has '*all too short a date*'. Unlike the weather, she does not change. The *"darling buds of May"* are shaken on the bushes, at the mercy of the wind, but she is steady and in control of herself and is '*more lovely and more temperate*'.

---

[59] Village bicycles are undeniably useful and are much coveted symbols of status in some cultures, but not all.

[60] R. Kelly's girlfriend might be forgiven for questioning the relationship he has with his Lexus Coupe; however, she can take comfort from the fact that if he's never pissed on the Lexus' leather seats, he must love her more. (Rumours suggest that R. Kelly enjoys peeing on his loved ones...could be a territorial thing).

[61] All too often, the summer is a cruel bastard, promising you a day of punting, picnics, and Pimm's by the river, only to capsize your boat, treat your picnic like a tart (blowing its red and white checked skirt into the air), and dilute your Pimm's with rainwater (thus effeminising a drink that was not particularly manly to begin with).

Now 'temperate' is a tricky word that the Manly Man should use with care. In Shakespeare's day, to describe a person as being temperate was to commend their mastery of their desires and emotions. A temperate lady was somebody prudent in all things; somebody who led 'the good life', and while not terribly likely to hop on the good foot and do the bad thing, they were considered to be a 'good egg'. A temperate person drinks in moderation and has the wisdom to carry out a thorough health and safety assessment before doing anything reckless, like jumping into bed with a stranger. If you are chatting up somebody in a nightclub during happy hour, there's a good chance that temperance may not be the best compliment to go for. Using temperance as a compliment in the wrong context (e.g. after the recipient of your chat-up line has just downed their 6th Tequila) could render the subject confused at best, and insulted at worst.[62] It is conceivable that somebody feckless and impulsive might consider temperance a compliment, but only if they could be sure that you were not taking the piss.

Lines 5-8

Sometime too hot the eye of heaven shines,....And often is his gold complexion dimm'd;....And every fair from fair sometime declines,....By chance, or nature's changing course, untrimm'd

After re-iterating the fickleness of the sun (*'the eye of heaven'*), which can blow hot and cold, beating down upon us relentlessly or becoming *'dimm'd'* as the weather and seasons change, Shakespeare muses on the transience of beauty and the

---

[62] 'You're a bit frigid' is probably not a great chat-up line, and girls have long gotten wise to the art of reverse psychology.

inescapable force of time. Like it or not, time is the element in which we live and, unless you are Marty McFly or Doctor Who, you have no control over it. Just as the weather changes from summer to autumn, our lives and appearances change as we grow older. *'Fair from fair sometime declines'* and beauty will fade. The object of Shakespeare's affections, like everything else (including the Earth itself), will change and age, day after day, as the sun rolls through the heavens.

But time is not the only element that brings about change. Fate and its array of mishaps and accidents is always lurking in the background. It is in the nature of things that the unexpected can happen at any time and chance moments can suddenly change our lives forever. Accidents or illness can turn our lives on their head and radically change us from who we are now.[63] Even if we are lucky enough to avoid being ambushed by a sudden unexpected change, we will still gradually change and decline as time goes by.

So these lines expound the wisdom that all things, beautiful or otherwise, will eventually turn to crap, but in a poetic, noble sort of way. While reminding your lover that life is short and bad things can happen at any moment is a rather depressing message for a love poem, it might just be enough to throw them into an existentialist 'live-for-the-moment' frenzy and convince them to jump into a taxi back to yours.

Lines 9-14

But thy eternal summer shall not fade...Nor lose possession of that fair thou ow'st;...Nor shall Death brag thou wander'st in his shade,...When in

---

63 Unfortunately, few accidents change us for the better; you don't accidentally lose your disability or become sexier.

eternal lines to time thou grow'st;...So long as men can breathe or eyes can see,...So long lives this, and this gives life to thee.

In the last six lines, Shakespeare appears to suddenly remember that this is supposed to be a love poem designed to seduce his lover into showing him a bit of ankle. We realize that the only reason that Shakespeare has been gloomily dwelling on the transience of summer, beauty and all worldly things, is so that he can contrast them with his lover's '*eternal*', everlasting beauty. While it is in the nature of worldly things to age and decline, Shakespeare makes the outrageous claim that his lover's beauty will never fade!

Shakespeare reassures his lover that '*thy eternal summer shall not fade*'. He will remember his lover at their best, in an everlasting snapshot of beauty that will not fade like the sun in winter. Shakespeare even goes on to tell his lover that they will escape Death and '*in eternal lines to time thou grow'st*'.[64] Now, perhaps Shakespeare has gone too far by conferring immortality to his lover; after all, comparisons with other immortals like Dracula, zombies and Conor McCloud (of the clan McCloud)[65] are not particularly flattering.

However, the truth is that Shakespeare's lover has been immortalized...in the eternal lines of the poem that you are holding in your hands at this very moment. Shakespeare proves his love by capturing the beauty of his lover in this poem for eternity, and '*So long as men can breathe or eyes can see,...So long lives this, and this gives life to thee.*' Through this poem, written over three

---

[64] Here, Shakespeare is referring to the lines of the poem that his lover is reading, rather than the lines on their face that mark the passage of time.

[65] The immortal warrior from Highlander, portrayed in an Oscar-worthy performance by Christopher Lambert who excellently captured the little known French-Scottish accent of Medieval Scotland.

hundred years ago, Shakespeare's lover is brought back to life; once again, he or she is alive and young and beautiful. Words do not decline or decay with time. *So long lives this* poem and for as long as people read it (as you just have), they will live on. Each time the poem is read, his lover's youth and beauty are recreated. They are in the prime of life forever.[66]

And here, Shakespeare shares the secret to the ultimate compliment; it is simply not enough to shower your lover with florid praise and empty platitudes, the trick is to demonstrate your love for them through your actions.

Sonnet 18 is the ultimate lesson in how to make your lover feel special. Shakespeare teaches us that the very least we can do is take the time to come up with an original and heartfelt compliment that goes beyond flattery. The Manly Man knows that a good compliment is an honest appreciation of who their lover is and what they are about. He takes the time to listen to his lover and understand their hopes and fears; armed with this knowledge, he motivates them to achieve their goals and reminds them that they have what it takes to deal with their worries. Shakespeare even went as far as to help his lover overcome any fear of dying by making them immortal.

When words fail him, or fail to do to his lover justice, the Manly Man shows his devotion through action! He writes a poem or builds a bridge in his lover's honour....or simply does the vacuuming so that his lover doesn't have to walk around the house with bits of Blu Tack and toy soldiers stuck to their feet.[67]

---

66 Much like the ancient photograph she used for her Facebook profile.

67 While some folk will buck you for a bag of chips and a can of coke, the love of your life is more likely to sleep with you in return for immortalizing them in a poem (and a bag of chips).

At the very least, the Manly Man endeavours to prove his love, and improve the life of his lover, through encouragement and action, regardless of whether he gets to see their rhyming couplets or not.

Manlifesto: The Manly Man knows that a good compliment should be heartfelt, sincere and original. More than that, he knows that the best compliments are delivered through actions rather than words. He shows his devotion through monumental acts of love, such as writing poems, building palaces, or even letting his lover hold the remote control now and again.

Lullaby

W. H. Auden

Poetry deals with the big things in life: birth, death, marriage, the passing of time, and how much quince an owl and a pussy cat can wrap in a five pound note. This particular poem, *Lullaby,* deals with that old favourite of palm-reading gypsies, Jilly Cooper and Jesus: love.

This poem is a meditation on love, and the brevity and transience of life's beautiful moments. It argues that love on a human level adds shimmer and meaning to our existence. Above all, this poem is a reminder to us that life is too short to not be having sex.

Lullaby

Lay your sleeping head, my love,
Human on my faithless arm;
Time and fevers burn away
Individual beauty from
Thoughtful children, and the grave
Proves the child ephemeral:
But in my arms till break of day
Let the living creature lie,
Mortal, guilty, but to me
The entirely beautiful.

Soul and body have no bounds:

To lovers as they lie upon
Her tolerant enchanted slope
In their ordinary swoon,
Grave the vision Venus sends
Of supernatural sympathy,
Universal love and hope;
While an abstract insight wakes
Among the glaciers and the rocks
The hermit's carnal ecstasy.

Certainty, fidelity
On the stroke of midnight pass
Like vibrations of a bell
And fashionable madmen raise
Their pedantic boring cry:
Every farthing of the cost,
All the dreaded cards foretell,
Shall be paid, but from this night
Not a whisper, not a thought,
Not a kiss nor look be lost.

Beauty, midnight, vision dies:
Let the winds of dawn that blow
Softly round your dreaming head
Such a day of welcome show
Eye and knocking heart may bless,
Find our mortal world enough;
Noons of dryness find you fed
By the involuntary powers,
Nights of insult let you pass
Watched by every human love.

Stanza 1

Lay your sleeping head, my love,...Human on my faithless arm;...Time and fevers burn away...Individual beauty from...Thoughtful children, and the grave,...Proves the child ephemeral:...But in my arms till break of day...Let the living creature lie,...Mortal, guilty, but to me...The entirely beautiful.

This poem is written in four stanzas, each one a complete sentence, ten lines long. Despite the length of these sentences and its sleep-inducing title, *Lullaby* is not designed to send us off to the Land of Nod; rather, this poem offers us a moment of perfection and tranquillity amidst our everyday preoccupations.

The beginning of the poem paints a scene of naughtiness: a bed on which two lovers lie. It is difficult to think of a more private and intimate moment. As one lover sleeps, the other lies awake reflecting upon the mysteries of love, such as how to reconcile a good night's sleep with a permanent 'hard-on'.

Rather than getting carried away in the fanciful language of the worst kind of love poetry, this poem stays down to earth. The sleeping lover is not depicted as some kind of god.[68] They are '*human*'. So too, is the lover narrating the poem. He will not promise great feats to prove his fidelity, but recognizes that he is faithless. However, he does not have the carry-on, nudge-nudge, wink-wink faithlessness of notorious manwhore Henry VIII, but has a lack of faith far more profound and befitting of the Manly Man: he knows that it is folly to have faith in the permanence of the moment that he is currently experiencing...it will not last.

The lover knows that '*Time and fevers burn away...Individual*

---

68 Presumably they fart in their sleep and leave a trail of drool on their pillow.

beauty...'. Familiarity diminishes our feeling of excitement faster than that of an adolescent ripping through his first copy of *Playboy.* Time changes everything and will take away the beauty of body and mind. The lover's thoughts follow this to its logical conclusion: 'the grave'. Death is the ultimate fun-sucker; the killjoy whose appearance makes the heart sink and brings lively conversations to a sudden end.[69]

Compared to 'the *grave*', which will be there for eternity, our brief lives are *'ephemeral'*; they pass by in an instant. The lover's morbid thoughts are stirred by the intensity of the current situàtion. Physical contact with their partner brings them face to face with the transience of things, but their thoughts also turn to the immediacy of the situation. The lover is holding someone whose mortality he recognises but whose physical beauty gives the moment a feeling of completeness and substance in the whirligig of time. He is torn between an existential reverie and the knowledge that life is too short not to be having sex right now.

Stanza 2

Soul and body have no bounds:...To lovers as they lie upon...Her tolerant enchanted slope...In their ordinary swoon,...Grave the vision Venus sends...Of supernatural sympathy,... Universal love and hope;...While an abstract insight wakes...Among the glaciers and the rocks...The hermit's carnal ecstasy.

The lover is appreciating an enchanted moment; a time of magic,

---

[69] Try as we might, we cannot avoid the Reaper; he is the greatest stalker in the world and on Facebook. One day Death will come knocking on our door. Even though he may bring some buns, or a nice slice of apple tart, don't be fooled into letting him in; that guy is a real drag!

as if a spell has been cast over himself and his lover. They will push the boundaries of earthly pleasure (which begin to go a bit wobbly around page 69 of *The Karma Sutra* – 'The Brahman's Tantric Cock-Hover [BTCH]') and in so doing may experience a new kind of spiritual awareness, along with some light chaffing. Boundaries between the physical and spiritual seem to vanish as they learn to reach new heights of physical and emotional ecstasy. Venus, the goddess of love, so impressed to see mere mortals attempt the 'BTCH', looks down upon them with benevolence and allows them their *'ordinary swoon'*. It is ordinary because the lovers are human and mortal, subject to the passing of time and sports injuries.

Being in love gives a vision of supernatural sympathy, universal love and hope that is common to lovers, but difficult to share with the rest of the world outside the bedroom. The watching lover suspects that at its heart, love may be a selfish thing that can only be experienced in an individual way. He is likened to a religious hermit; wise and worldly, but perhaps a bit of a wanker (owing to his solitary lifestyle). He lives in a remote and harsh landscape, where he seeks to break down the boundary between the physical and the spiritual through isolation and suffering. The lover's ecstasy too, might simply be selfish; he could be exploiting another to help him explore a heightened level of emotional experience, share the rent, and perhaps do the odd spot of ironing.

Stanza 3

Certainty, fidelity…On the stroke of midnight pass…Like vibrations of a bell…And fashionable madmen raise…Their pedantic boring cry:… Every farthing of the cost,…All the dreaded cards foretell,…Shall be paid, but from this night…Not a whisper, not a thought,…Not a kiss nor look be lost.

Any fixed notions that we can have faith in *'on the stroke of midnight pass'*. Love's mysterious spell has replaced the perceived 'truth' of things laid down for us by *'fashionable madmen'* who claim to know what is right and wrong. These zealots have fixed ideas about how other people should live their lives and believe that they have a right to legislate what is morally right for the rest of us.[70]

However, moral notions, like fashions, change over time and place.[71] Each era has its share of ranting madmen, mealy-mouthed hypocrites who tell us what to believe and how to behave; and then light up their opium or crack pipe (time dependent) to get a good buzz going before they head off to watch a hanging, or have sex with their cousin (again, era/country specific).

For the lover in the poem, the ideas and rhetoric of the moralists are nothing more than a *'pedantic boring cry'*. He is in a special place where time operates differently and where mystery exists; however, he knows that the spell will soon be broken and that a price will have to be paid for this stolen time, and *'paid down to the last farthing'*. Perhaps the lover sleeping by his side is married. Maybe they have had a few too many drinks and morning will shed light on the harsh reality of their situation. If the price to be paid is going to be high, then each second should be spent well; spent with passion. *"Pssssssst. Are you asleep? I say. Pssssst…."*

---

[70] These *'fashionable madmen'* (or *'madpersons'* to be more politically correct) include politicians, theologians and that man in the park who insists that he is the reincarnation of Joan of Arc.

[71] Burning witches seemed like a good idea at the time, but nowadays banning witches from social media is a more appropriate (and perhaps harsher) punishment.

Stanza 4

Beauty, midnight, vision dies:...Let the winds of dawn that blow...Softly round your dreaming head...Such a day of welcome show...Eye and knocking heart may bless,... Find our mortal world enough;...Noons of dryness find you fed...By the involuntary powers,... Nights of insult let you pass...Watched by every human love.

At last the spell is broken. Dawn breaks, and as the darkness lightens, the lover makes a wish: that the coming days be welcoming and the ordinary world be enough. In the knocking heart of the guilty lovers, the knowledge of this night together might find them peace. The wish is unspoken but it is made with a generosity of feeling that banishes the previous doubts that love is a selfish thing. The ordinary world of the mundane might be made bearable not by any political formula or religious creed, but by the knowledge of love on a human level.

Now, if this poem does not justify a robust, proactive, and thorough approach to finding love, then we don't know what does. It is much to the disservice of the Manly Man that this difficult and discriminating process is misconstrued as 'manwhoring' by its critics. This is unfair because, whether we admit it or not, Manly Men are always in search of the *one*: the best person to settle down with and maybe even have children. The Manly Man knows that there is no point cheating on an unwanted lover; time is short and we will not waste our time or anyone else's.

So, Manly Men, go forth and know love on a human level. (I hear that there are websites and mobile applications to assist you in this honourable endeavour).

Manlifesto: The Manly Man is mindful of the present and appreciative of what he has. He has learned from the wisdom of Buddha and the science of Drs. Killingworth and Gilbert and knows that a wandering mind is an unhappy mind. [72] So, it's best to devote his time to something that's easy to focus on...like the naked profile of a lover for example. [73]

---

[72] A study of mind wandering and happiness in 2250 volunteers revealed that people spend 47% of their time thinking about something other than what they're actually doing. More importantly, the study demonstrated that people were significantly less happy when their minds were wandering than when they were not...regardless of what they were doing (even vacuuming). Incidentally, it's worth noting that people's minds wandered least during sex (10% of the time). Source: Killingsworth MA, Gilbert DT. A wandering mind is an unhappy mind. Science 2010; 330: 932.

[73] The Manly Man has also learned from Aesop's fable of *The Dog and the Bone(r)*. In this fable, a dog with a bone(r) sees the reflection of itself in the river with a bigger bone(r) and dives into the water; the dog ends up losing the bone(r) it had in the pursuit of one that did not exist. Wisdom!

The Voice

Thomas Hardy

This poem is about heartbreak, that swift kick in the ventricles that all men, even the manly, receive at some stage in their lives. Unfortunately, being manly is not always the same as being good-looking. You only need to compare Elvis to Winston Churchill to realise that, as attractive a concept as manliness may be, it rarely translates into physical beauty. Some of the most Manly Men, the world-shapers, the great artists, philosophers and scientists, were just so because they were a bit on the ropey-looking side. Marx, Darwin, and Tolkien[74] were not famous for having to fight off admirers, which meant they could devote more time to the theories of economics, evolution and the geopolitical situation in Mordor.

These Manly Men elevated themselves above desire and heartbreak by throwing themselves into their work. They devoted themselves to the greater good, the betterment of humanity, and if in doing so they were able to show the misguided fool who dumped them what they were missing out on, then so much the better. Newton developed his theory of gravity just to spite some lady who spurned his advances, and while Mr Betamax can go screw himself, many ex-lovers have lived to regret dumping Mr Kindle. The author of this poem, Thomas Hardy, was no stranger

---

[74] Many of these men were complete hornballs, randy little buggers with little other than *Big Jugs Monthly* and a box of Kleenex to satisfy them. Einstein's theory of relativity was a wank he did not have, and Alexander Graham Bell turned smut into the telephone...., which, years later, would be turned back into smut on the telephone. (SuperSexlineChat Tel 097555321).

to heartache and in this poem he teaches us how to man up, move on and make stuff. For an essay on how to turn lost love into world-changing theories or a nice set of shelves, read on.

The Voice

Woman much missed, how you call to me, call to me,
Saying that now you are not as you were
When you had changed from the one who was all to me,
But as at first, when our day was fair.

Can it be you that I hear? Let me view you, then,
Standing as when I drew near to the town
Where you would wait for me: yes, as I knew you then,
Even to the original air-blue gown!

Or is it only the breeze in its listlessness
Travelling across the wet mead to me here,
You being ever dissolved to wan wistlessness,
Heard no more again far or near?

Thus I; faltering forward,
Leaves around me falling,
Wind oozing thin through the thorn from norward,
And the woman calling.

Stanza 1

Woman much missed, how you call to me, call to me,...Saying that now you are not as you were...When you had changed from the one who was all to me,...But as at first, when our day was fair.

The titular *'Voice'* of this poem is that of a woman echoing in the memory of the poet; it is the voice of lost love. In the first stanza the words *'call to me'* are repeated like an echo forever repeating in the chambers of the poet's mind. The poet hears the voice of a lost love; she is telling him that the past can be recreated, that she can once again be the centre of everything he holds dear. She calls, and he recalls, again and again their past love as it was at the beginning, long before his heart turned sea-sick green and his hopes wilted like spinach.

Stanza 2

Can it be you that I hear? Let me view you, then,...Standing as when I drew near to the town...Where you would wait for me: yes, as I knew you then,...Even to the original air-blue gown!

'Can it be you that I hear?' The poet wonders why he can hear, but not see, his old lover. Nostalgia is playing silly-buggers with his senses. The key moments of our lives,[75] good and bad, are recaptured through powerful and lasting sensations so that we can relive them in our imagination; a sudden scent of perfume on the air can instantly bring us back to the first time we smelled it; the song that played during your first romantic fumbling transports you back to that magic moment;[76] or most disappointing of all, we can wake from a dream in which the break-up with our lover never happened, only to remember that they have gone, leaving nothing behind but a sexy, ghostly memory traced in 'ectoplasm' upon the bedclothes.

---

[75] The *really* important, Match-of-the-Day-highlights-important moments.
[76] Songs like 'Oh Little Town of Bethlehem' and 'Agadoo' in the cases of your humble, but Manly, authors.

In the poet's imagination, the voice transforms into the image of his old lover waiting; a figure of beauty and hope and expectation that fills the clear blue air. The uncomplicated innocence of new love and the excitement of their first greeting still have a powerful hold on the poet's mind. The optimism of love is exclaimed in a moment of joyous recollection. He remembers the vivid details of how she looked and the '*air-blue gown*' she wore. For a moment, the past is captured and brought to life once again.

Stanza 3

Or is it only the breeze in its listlessness...Travelling across the wet mead to me here,...You being ever dissolved to wan wistlessness,...Heard no more again far or near?

The third stanza begins with the ominous word 'Or'; this word raises doubts, and the clear image of hope and love starts to waver and change. This long, slow sentence reflects the poet's mood of hopelessness; the weather has darkened from the clear blue skies of before. Words like '*listlessness*" and '*wistlessness*' seem to sap all hope and energy out of the wet air, and the clear, bright image of the woman becomes blurred and indistinct in the bleak, autumnal landscape. The poet questions the reliability of his senses and the image of his love is '*dissolved*' by the wind and rain.

We are building up to a reality check: the lover has gone forever. The poet is left with nothing other than memories and a recent email just to let him know how great his lover's life has been ever since they left him: new boyfriend, new flat, and that dog he always wanted, all tempered by a most *sincere* wish that he, too, should find such bliss.

Will this be the last time the poet hears the voice? Will the chill of autumn bring on a final winter when the voice will be stilled forever? Will we all reach for our razor blades?

Stanza 4

Thus I; faltering forward,...Leaves around me falling,...Wind oozing thin through the thorn from norward,...And the woman calling.

The final stanza shakes us from the poet's reverie of the past and brings us back to the present, like the word 'sexplosion' in a conversation we were only half listening to. The semicolon after *'Thus I;'* stops us in mid-thought, the voice that had lured the poet into nostalgia for the past is silenced abruptly, and the poet is brought back to the here and now. The stark truth is that he is a man alone in a bleak landscape.

The future, whatever future remains, is uncertain. It is something that the poet now stumbles towards. The colours of summer have faded like the colour of the leaves and the fading memory of the voice. As the leaves fall, so too will the poet. Sharp thorns prick against the cold wind that will drain the life out of him, as will the memory of the voice that calls to him, a constant reminder of lost happiness.

However, Thomas Hardy does not ask us to pity him. He does not want us to reach for our handkerchiefs in some sort of emotional outpouring. He simply leaves us with the stark image of a man alone; a man trying to deal with the passing of time.

We see the poet's lonely figure, his long black overcoat fluttering in the wind; one man against the world. Den! Cut to a montage of Thomas Hardy tying on his Rambo-red bandana, assembling an Uzi 9mm, strapping a couple of Samurai swords to his back, and dusting down his knuckledusters. This time it's personal. Finally, suited and booted, our beat poet moves on, ready to beat the living hell out of disenchantment and poor rhyme scheme.

"What shall we do Thomas?"

"Fuck 'em!"

This poem lets us know that we are not alone in feeling… alone. All men face heartbreak at one time or another. What singles out the Manly Man is how he deals with it. The Manly Man takes heartbreak and channels it into greatness, for reasons noble or otherwise. In order to distract himself or exact revenge, the Manly Man composes 'Sweet Child o' Mine', he writes 'Anna Karenina', or in an act of phallic, Gallic defiance, he engineers a giant steel erection in the middle of Paris.

This poem also reminds us to spare a thought for all those lovers we may have jilted; the times you slinked your arm out from underneath a sleeping one-night stand like a Jedi Master; the Sunday mornings when you woke up in a strange house and felt compelled to nip out for a pint of 'get me the hell out of here!', leaving a heartbroken lover to choke on a comic-book dust cloud, a 'Meep! Meep!' ringing in their ears as you road-runnered the hell home.

Manlifesto: Rather than wallow in nostalgia, the Manly Man channels the pain of heartbreak into something productive; he throws himself into training, helping others or creating something new (but non-electrical; the Manly Man knows that a rogue tear could fershnicker the circuits).

Sonnet 130: My Mistress' Eyes Are Nothing like the Sun

William Shakespeare

The fact that this poem has the word *'mistress'* in its title tells us that it's about love, secret sexy time, or maybe even both if we're lucky. Nowadays, mistress is a word we associate with sleazy headlines from the tabloid press, dramas about politicians' naughty weekends away playing 'Doctors and Nurses' or 'Heads of European Banks and Chambermaids'. However, in this poem, Shakespeare is not beseeching his mistress to throw a leash around his neck and take him for a walk around London.[77] You see, in Shakespeare's day a mistress was a respected lady, and it seems that this particular mistress was worthy of having a poem written about her.

In this poem Shakespeare wants to let his mistress know that she is the object of his desire, the one person that he sets above all others, but he wants to do it without looking too desperate. This poem offers some sage advice to the Manly Man who wants to express the uniqueness of his love, without the use of worn-out clichés and sentimental claptrap. It teaches us how to flatter the love of our life like a gentleman poet, rather than an obsequious butt-kisser.[78]

---

[77] Followed by a game of 'Elizabethan Lord and Wench in Flame-Coloured Taffeta'.
[78] This will be particularly useful for those of you who are 'young, dumb, and full of ... the joys of blossoming love'.

118

My mistress' eyes are nothing like the sun (Sonnet No. 130)

My mistress' eyes are nothing like the sun;
Coral is far more red than her lips' red:
If snow be white, why then her breasts are dun;
If hairs be wires, black wires grow on her head.
I have seen roses damask'd, red and white,
But no such roses see I in her cheeks;
And in some perfumes is there more delight
Than in the breath that from my mistress reeks.
I love to hear her speak,--yet well I know
That music hath a far more pleasing sound;
I grant I never saw a goddess go,
My mistress when she walks, treads on the ground;
And yet, by heaven, I think my love as rare
As any she belied with false compare.

Lines 1-4

My mistress' eyes are nothing like the sun;...Coral is far more red than her lips' red:...If snow be white, why then her breasts are dun;...If hairs be wires, black wires grow on her head.

This poem is a sonnet of fourteen lines, written in three sentences. The opening sentence leaves us in no doubt that Shakespeare is going to avoid clichéd compliments and comparisons. The radiance of his mistress' eyes is nothing compared to that of the sun; the colour of her lips cannot compare with the deep-red of undersea coral; and her breasts are the colour of dun compared to the whiteness of snow.[79] It is almost as if Shakespeare has set out to insult his mistress rather than flatter her; or it could be that he would rather insult her appearance than her intelligence, because there are some wonders of Nature that nobody can overshadow; some comparisons are simply too absurd and unfair to make.[80]

The unflattering comparisons continue as Shakespeare compares his mistress' hair to black wires sprouting from her head. Maybe it's all about context. It could be that this was an excellent bit of silver-tongued chat back in the days before the mass manufacturing of wire. When this poem was written the production of wire was skilled and represented something closer to magic than industrial processing. Wire was made by heating up a bar of metal and then, when it was molten hot, drawing it apart until a thin strand of metal was formed between the two pieces. To produce wire of any length was very difficult, so wire was a valuable commodity.

Even still, Shakespeare could have compared his mistress' hair to gold or silver wire, which can be spun out to make delicate necklaces and jewellery; but instead of being gold, his mistress's hair is black; black and wiry, like Robocop's pubes.

Lines 5-8

I have seen roses damask'd, red and white,...But no such roses see I in her

---

[79] It is also worth emphasizing that when Shakespeare says his mistress' breasts are "dun", he is referring to their light brown colour, and not to the fact that her knockers are knackered; even Shakespeare, himself, could not poetry his way back out of that kind of abuse.

[80] For example, the lead character in Gregory David Roberts' book, *Shantaram*, says that his muse's eyes "were the colour of sand in the palm of your hand at sunset." Of course they were Gregory...of course they were.

cheeks;...And in some perfumes is there more delight ...Than in the breath that from my mistress reeks.

Perhaps Shakespeare is all romanced out after *Romeo and Juliet* and is blowing off some steam as the unflattering comparisons continue in the second sentence. To stick the boot in further, Shakespeare assures us that he is a good judge of what he sees and is not making these comparisons lightly. He appreciates the delicate beauty of damask needlework. The roses he describes refer to the heraldic symbols of two powerful political groups from Shakespeare's time and would have been a common decoration.[81] The rose is also a symbol of beauty, but Shakespeare makes it clear his mistress is no English Beauty; there are no roses *'in her cheeks'* and no scent of rose to cover the smell of her breath, which reeks apparently. This is particularly damning as a decent indicator of Love's sincerity is whether, early in the morning (hopefully after some romancing), you're prepared to thrust your tongue into a mouth that was filled with a donor kebab (or cheeseboard and pickles, depending how classy your date was), only the night before.[82]

Perhaps Shakespeare is simply embarking on a bit of frilly-collared 'negging', a cynical variation of 'treat them mean, keep them keen' that insecure men use to pick up women by undermining their self-esteem.[83] However, Shakespeare never

---

[81] The Houses of York and Lancaster were represented with white and red roses, respectively.

[82] Cher, the plastic-pouted poet laureate, knew this when she penned the timeless *Shoop Song*; "If you wanna know, if he loves you so, it's in his kiss...that's where it is!" (...so make him prove his Love by having blue cheese and marmite on garlic bread before you meet up).

[83] Manly Men know this dubious tactic of making the object of your desire feel a bit rubbish in order to make them glad of your attention (and more likely to get-off with you) is un-Manly and unethical; fortunately, people aren't stupid, and negging is more likely to secure your status as an insufferable knob-end than secure you any 'love'.

stoops to the vulgarity of 'that dress is really nice, my grandmother had one just like it last season.'

Lines 9-12

I love to hear her speak,--yet well I know...That music hath a far more pleasing sound;...I grant I never saw a goddess go,...My mistress when she walks, treads on the ground;

Up until now, it appears that this poem is a cruel attack on someone who Shakespeare despises, rather than a love song to the object of his desire. Each of the characteristics that Shakespeare might have praised, his mistress's eyes, lips, hair, boobies and complexion are all criticised rather than complimented. His mistress would have been well within her rights to rip up the poem in a fit of rage and withold sexy time indefinitely.

However, at the start of the next sentence it looks as though all might be redeemed and that Shakespeare is finally going to pick out the feature he has been waiting to praise; her voice perhaps? Yes, he loves to listen to her voice and yet it is not music to his ears! You see, her speech cannot compare to the *'pleasing sound'* of music; it's as simple as that![84]

Shakespeare steadfastly refuses to make exaggerated comparisons for the sake of making a good impression, even though that is what people expect from poets and lovers. He finishes his volley of abuse by saying that he's pretty sure that his

---

[84] This is particularly pertinent in Greece, where one turns from the bar to ask the chain-smoking, elderly gentleman to stop screaming in your ear, only to find a beautiful woman talking to her friends; fortunately for Greek women, most men are rendered deaf by beauty.

mistress is not a goddess,[85] even though he has never seen one; his mistress *'treads on the ground'* and can't even hover, which is a prerequisite for any budding goddess.

Lines 13-14

And yet, by heaven, I think my love as rare…As any she belied with false compare.

In the last two lines, Shakespeare finally reveals where his thoughts have been leading to, and the entire sentiment of the poem is turned on its head. Everything that has gone before is shed in a new light. Shakespeare has not placed his mistress upon a pedestal of fanciful comparisons, nor viewed her through the distorting lens of all-consuming love, because he loves her for who she is, a real person who farts when she laughs too hard and occasionally misses the odd nasal hair. Shakespeare's realistic perception of his mistress does not diminish the intensity of his feelings for her, but rather it intensifies them.

It is the very flesh and bones of his mistress that Shakespeare loves. He strips away all sentimentality and overblown comparisons. What remains is a love that is powerful in its integrity; a love that is more than skin deep. The froth of superficial flattery has been replaced by the expression of true appreciation for another human being. Shakespeare's mistress may not be a goddess, but she has been immortalized in the lines of this poem.

When you're in love, the sun shines brighter, the post office queues are shorter, and you're less likely to change the radio

---

[85] And a good thing too because those chicks require a lot of sacrifice.

station when Phil Collins comes on; you think twice about adding a Jaegerbomb to every pint because your senses are already heightened and you don't want to deaden them with the artificial buzz of alcohol. In this poem, Shakespeare warns us that Love can be as hallucinogenic as crack cocaine or toad sweat.[86] He urges the Manly Man to be stoic in the face of Love and to accept our lovers despite their faults, as it's these imperfections that make them special.

The Manly Man knows that Love can cloud his judgement with delusions that are bad for the lover, the loved and everyone in their circle. Therefore, the Manly Man does not confer unrealistic attributes to his lover and so is not surprised and devastated when the illusion slips. He understands that it is unreasonable to expect a partner to live up to unrealistic expectations,[87] and that the pressure to meet these expectations can make his partner miserable. The Manly Man is aware that Love can turn even the most well-meaning of men into a selfish bollocks who turns his back on his friends, family and even his football team. Despite all this, the Manly Man recognizes that the heightened sensory experience of Love is something to be savoured and treasured, just not at the cost of his sanity.

Manlifesto: The Manly Man knows that Love is a wonderful drug, but is aware that it comes with serious side effects, including selfishness and delusion. He celebrates his partner's imperfections, because he knows that if their farts really smelled of roses, a *Dutch oven*[88] would be far less intimate.

---

86 He would have added a line about it being as addictive as Tetris, too, if they'd had Gameboys back in the 16th Century.
87 And dangerous; nobody can hold a fart in for 24 h.
88 Interesting sexual manoeuvre during which one lover forces the other beneath the bed covers to smell their fart.

Neutral Tones

Thomas Hardy

We sincerely hope that the sentiments expressed in this poem are new to you, and that you have never yet in your Manly life been touched by heartbreak. However, given the Manly Man's propensity for buckling their swash and getting themselves covered in daring do, we suspect that such hopes will be in vain. This poem is a sad homage to life long after 'funstroke'.[89] It is about love ground into dust[90] and passion piddled away to ashen sludge.

Should a Manly Man ever find himself on the pointy end of heartache, this poem is a reminder that they are not alone. It offers the consolation that many men have survived heartache and gone on to better things. The heart is a muscle and Manly Men know that breaking down muscle only serves to make it grow back stronger. (Unless your heartache is accompanied by a shooting pain down the left-hand side of your body, in which case you're probably having a heart attack and should consult a doctor rather than a poetry book).

Neutral Tones

We stood by a pond that winter day,
And the sun was white, as though chidden of God,

---

[89]The psychological affliction whereby a man is blinded to a woman's faults by her scintillating conversation and ability to look smashing in athletic wear.
[90]And not in a good way: in Spanish "*hacemos un polvete*" means let's make dust, a euphemism for a strenuous bump and grind. May your life be blessed with more bumping than grinding!

And a few leaves lay on the starving sod,
--They had fallen from an ash, and were gray.

Your eyes on me were as eyes that rove
Over tedious riddles solved years ago;
And some words played between us to and fro--
On which lost the more by our love.

The smile on your mouth was the deadest thing
Alive enough to have strength to die;
And a grin of bitterness swept thereby
Like an ominous bird a-wing....

Since then, keen lessons that love deceives,
And wrings with wrong, have shaped to me
Your face, and the God-curst sun, and a tree,
And a pond edged with grayish leaves.

Stanza 1

We stood by a pond that winter day,....And the sun was white, as though chidden of God,....And a few leaves lay on the starving sod,....--They had fallen from an ash, and were gray.

This poem is written in four dollops of melancholy: four stanzas with four lines in each. It starts off as though it is going to follow the once-upon-a-time-happily-ever-after-y of a typical love poem with the poet and his lover standing by a pond, late in the afternoon on a sunny winter's day; however, the sun, usually used to add a warm fuzzy glow to proceedings, is a cold, white disc. It has turned pale, '*as though chidden*' (or given a light bollocking) by God and gives no warmth to the bleak landscape. Starved of sunlight, everything is frozen and dead. The ground is barren and hard and all the nutrients have leached from the fallen leaves that lie in a grey carpet of ash around the trees. The colourlessness of the scene reflects the dying affection that the couple once had for one another. All of the strands of love (trust, passion, fun, and security), once colourful and bright as a brand new packet of Plastercine, have been rolled into a confused, brown mess of emotion.

Given that most people have been programmed to get bored easily, many Manly Men will be familiar with this sentiment of waning love. A love that elects to go to the cinema, just so that it doesn't have to make polite conversation anymore. Most of us have experienced those sad moments, sat in awkward silence, wishing that our partner would just GO AWAY! Or worse still, moments when we have tried to melt the frostiness away with a joke, only for our charms to be irritably shrugged off, and we realise that it is *she* who wants us to just GO AWAY! Times when her fluorescent-green Slush Puppy seems to be laced with Kryptonite against our superhuman charm, stripping away the false virtues and attributes that she once cloaked us in, and doing irreparable damage to her libido. The naked truth hits home and we're left feeling like a fraud.

Stanza 2

Your eyes on me were as eyes that rove,...Over tedious riddles solved years ago;...And some words played between us to and fro--...On which lost the more by our love.

As the poet reflects on this sad scene, the image of his ex-lover is clear in his imagination. Her eyes that once looked into his own with love and without self-consciousness (a rare privilege extended to lovers and psychopaths), now look at him with boredom and disinterest. The words the couple now exchange 'to and fro' between one another are superficial. Conversations that in the past would have been exciting, now seem dull and meaningless. This contrast heightens the sense of emptiness that exists now; their words are sounds without meaning compared to the meaningful silences of before.

The only thing more awkward than the silence that enshrouds a doomed relationship, are the few words exchanged. Shaped and sharpened by disenchantment, this prose of antipathy is like cut-glass, designed to belittle the ex-lover and slash away their pride. Disenchanted lovers are like tennis players, serving up well-timed volleys of abuse in a bid to score points off one another. This is bad enough when done in private, but even worse when played out before an audience of friends. We have all been in the uncomfortable situation of watching a couple exchange snide comments and deprecating gestures, rolling their eyes (or simply just doing the wanker sign, depending how classy your friends are) to let us know just how much of a wanker their partner is.[91]

Stanza 3

The smile on your mouth was the deadest thing...Alive enough to have strength to die;...And a grin of bitterness swept thereby...Like an ominous bird a-wing....

In this long, unfinished sentence, the poet remembers with aching clarity how he watched the joy and love drain from

---

[91] Which really just makes them look like a wanker for staying with the wanker for so long. Wankers!

everything, including his lover's smile: not only has the sun gone cold and his scintillating chit-chat become tedious, but even the smile that used to light-up his lover's face has died. It is now a cynical, bitter smile that hangs in the air '*like an ominous bird*', less like *Big Bird* and more like one of those freaky-beaky fellows from the *Dark Crystal*; a vulture picking over the bones of their dead relationship. The bleak image of his ex-lover's smile will be fixed in the mind of the poet forever. While this image is indeed very poignant, it should be pointed out that there's nothing terribly alluring about grim, loveless smiles. This haunting image should serve to make the Manly Man grateful that he is no longer making love to *Mumm-Ra* from the *Thunder Cats*.

Stanza 4

Since then, keen lessons that love deceives,...And wrings with wrong, have shaped to me...Your face, and the God-curst sun, and a tree,...And a pond edged with grayish leaves.

In the final stanza we are brought back to the present moment. '*Since then*', the poet has learned the harsh '*keen lessons that love deceives*'. Love adds colour and vibrancy to the everyday, it makes life's tribulations bearable and offers hope for the future. Love promises to be pure and undying; it promises to always laugh at your jokes and never fart under the bedclothes. When love dies, it threatens to take away the *Technicolor, Wizard-of-Oz* texture of the world, leaving behind a grey, limp approximation of the real thing. Many poets would build upon this theme of disenchanted love and leave us with a gushing over-sentimental finale. However, Thomas Hardy is not a 'poor-me' poet; rather, he is a 'shit-happens-get-on-with-it' merchant. He simply leaves us with the image of a dead love that has been burned into his memory:

the sun, a tree, a pond, grey leaves, and a bitter smile. The poet has been there and shares the experience with honesty and sincerity; a bleak, neutral image in our mind's eye.

The message that love can die is sad to be sure, but it's reassuring to know that the same sort of disappointments have happened to poets and rock stars, from Thomas Hardy to Axl Rose. We can take solace from their delicate meditations on lost love, from poems such as *Neutral Tones* and songs like 'I used to love her, but I had to kill her' by *Guns and Roses*.

No matter how bleak things appear, the Manly Man knows that the world is still beautiful; he knows that heartbreak and disappointments can change his perception of the world, but not the world itself. It's how the Manly Man reacts to dead love and romantic mishaps that is important. The Manly Man tries to be objective in the face of an emotional thunderstorm. He knows that sometimes love just fizzles out without it being anyone's fault. In some cases love, like life, can become just a habit; dying love can just hang in there for the sake of it, despite the pathetic quality of its existence. It takes a Manly Man to know when to (metaphorically)[92] put a pillow over its face and move on.

Manlifesto: The Manly Man recognizes when a relationship is over, faces that truth and moves on. He knows that despite heartbreak, the world is still beautiful, sunsets still awe-inspiring and cats falling into fish tanks still hilarious.

---

[92] And we really do mean metaphorically; we cannot over-emphasize, just how metaphorical this sentiment is.

Part 5. Nature: Not just a place where large numbers of ducks fly by overhead uncooked

The World Is Too Much with Us

William Wordsworth

Tonka Trucks, lawn mowers, lion taming and an obsession with chainsaws, betray the fact that we have always been fascinated by our apparent dominion over Nature. In the most extreme manifestation of our flagrant abuse of power over the Earth, we are simply happy to move bits of it about for no apparent reason in order show it who is boss (any excuse to rent a JCB and a skip). The problem is that we are intimately connected to the natural processes going on around us and cannot manipulate the natural world without consequences. William Wordsworth wrote this poem over 200 years ago to remind people that they are part of the natural world and should treat it with more care.

Although Wordsworth could never have envisioned our nightmare world in which the land is scoured and crumpled during the extraction of materials for making fidget spinners and selfie sticks, he foresaw many of the environmental dilemmas we now face. This poem is a warning from the past that we have yet to heed: if Nature is the source of Life and Happiness, we would do well to enjoy it rather than try (and succeed) to piss it off all the time.[93]

The World Is Too Much With Us

The world is too much with us; late and soon,

---

[93] While *The World Is Too Much with Us* is a warning of the impact of civilization and the impeding industrial revolution upon *Nature*, the next poem, *London* by William Blake, considers how these things affect *people* and *society*.

Getting and spending, we lay waste our powers:
Little we see in nature that is ours;
We have given our hearts away, a sordid boon!
This Sea her bosom to the moon;
The Winds that will be howling at all hours
And are up-gathered now like sleeping flowers;
For this, for every thing, we are out of tune;
It moves us not. Great God! I'd rather be
A Pagan suckled in a creed outworn;
So might I, standing on this pleasant lea,
Have glimpses that would make me less forlorn;
Have sight of Proteus coming from the sea;
Or hear old Triton blow his wreathed horn.

Lines 1-4

The world is too much with us; late and soon,…Getting and spending, we lay waste our powers:…Little we see in nature that is ours;…We have given our hearts away, a sordid boon!

This poem is in the form of a sonnet comprised of fourteen lines arranged into four sentences (get down and give me 40 press ups if you can't recognise a sonnet by now). It was written when Great Britain was becoming the great industrial powerhouse of the world. The refinement of the steam engine and development of canals, railways and steamships would soon make it possible to manufacture and transport vast quantities of goods all over the country, and then all over the world. Britain was becoming wealthy, and wealth encourages more and more consumption, something we know all about today. Right from the onset of the Industrial Revolution, William Wordsworth warned of the consequences of chopping down forests, ripping coal and

133

minerals out of the ground in order to build and fuel bigger and bigger factories; a warning that many of us have yet to listen to.

In the first line, *'The world is too much with us; late and soon'*, Wordsworth is referring not to the world of nature, but the world of materialism in which nature is seen as a resource to be mined, quarried and built upon. Through this viewpoint, and the pursuit of material gain, *'we lay waste our powers'* to appreciate the beauty of the natural world as it is. Our ability to be awestruck by the power and beauty of nature diminishes as we continue to turn it into man-made beauty.

While we should be impressed with mankind's initiative and capacity for invention (flat screen TVs, smart phones and clap-on clap-off lights are all amazing feats of engineering), it is important to remember that many of these new technologies will soon be considered rubbish and obsolete (few people remember the ZX Spectrum and Betamax... 'Alexa, watch this space'). Technological developments have the potential to create jobs and prosperity (in the sexy parts of the World anyway); however, the search for more precious metals, semi-conductors, and elements needed to build this technology, leads to the destruction of the natural resources in which these materials are hidden.

Perhaps if we had to use butterfly wing-nuts or a rare testicular mineral such as buffalo scrotonium to make microchips, maybe even the most die-hard techno geek would sympathise with Nature, and think twice, before indulging in the latest HD-ready-George Foreman-smartphone-meat-toaster. Do we really need to mass produce integrated technologies that hook-up everything but our scrotum to a mobile phone?[94] Digital connectivity comes at the price of being disconnected to Nature.

---

[94] Although, we believe that iPhone are working on an App: MapMyBallbag

Wordsworth warns that *'We have given our hearts away'*; we have exchanged natural order for material convenience and have lost our connection with Nature as part of the transaction. With equal measures of greed and arrogance we think that we can exert our own will upon Nature, bend it towards an industrial revolution that will march into a future of never ending gifts. For Wordsworth, the deal we have done is a grubby and *'sordid boon!'*; we grub around in the dirt to tear away its riches.

Lines 5-8

This Sea her bosom to the moon;...The Winds that will be howling at all hours...And are up-gathered now like sleeping flowers;...For this, for every thing, we are out of tune;

Wordsworth goes on to describe the great elemental forces of nature, such as the sea and the wind. Nature operates its own system of equilibrium and balance that stretches from the monumental interactions between the Earth and the Moon to the delicate processes that give rise to flowers and hummingbird toenails. Nature is constantly regulating itself in a vast and complex pattern. The moon controls the tides and the tides are whipped up by strong winds. The wind also creates music as it blows through tree branches or the strings of an Aeolian harp.[95] All is constantly changing, yet all remains in constant harmony.

Only we strike a discordant note!

In the opinion of the poet, we have exchanged the melody of

---

[95] Aeolian harps work by stretching strings across a long box. When the box is placed somewhere where the wind can blow across it, like under the frame of a sash window, or beneath the toilet seat of an Indian restaurant, a strange music is produced.

nature for the flatulent clatter of machinery. *'Great God!'* exclaims Wordsworth. How has it come to this?

Lines 9-14

It moves us not. Great God! I'd rather be...A Pagan suckled in a creed outworn;...So might I, standing on this pleasant lea,...Have glimpses that would make me less forlorn;...Have sight of Proteus coming from the sea;...Or hear old Triton blow his wreathed horn.

In the last six lines, Wordsworth moves his eco-friendly argument on, concluding that he would rather be an old-world Pagan who appreciates nature than a modern-day Christian who does not. During the Industrial Revolution (and ever since), the Church of England stayed quiet in the face of rampant capitalism, which is probably not surprising for a religion that preaches mankind's dominion over the Earth. Wordsworth would rather have been brought up in an ancient religion that still held nature as something sacred; one that promotes dancing naked in the moonlight and the odd wine-fuelled orgy.

Like some ancient Greek, Wordsworth dreams of standing in a meadow, watching the god *'Proteus coming from the sea'* or hearing the great sea-god *'Triton blow his wreathed horn'*. Wordsworth does not merely throw in a few impressive names from the Classics to add gravitas to the poem (so that we all throw our knickers at him), but is harking back to a golden age when men were still in tune with their environment;[96] a simple, yet heroic time when Nature included us in her embrace; a time when listening to and

---

[96] Even if it would take a few more centuries before they got in touch with their Manly-yet-feminine side).

appreciating the earth was more important than over-exploiting it in order to make a few quid.

Nowadays, we are constantly bombarded with fake news and misinformation about both sides of environmental arguments. On one side we're being made to feel guilty all the time and on the other we're being encouraged to take the piss out of people who chain themselves to trees and subscribe to *The Composters Post*. There is a confused garble of environmental outrage from the media which gobble up trees and electricity in order to tell us how naughty we are for wasting resources on one page, and then urge us to buy a 4x4 on the next. And if the truth be told, the only climate change that politicians really care about is that of the political climate, as they flip-flop from one policy position to the next.

Press and politicians try to turn the Manly Man and his hippy tree-hugger brother against one another. On one hand, they portray the Manly Man as a petrol-headed, eco-phobic, plastic-container-dumping, insecticide-snorting idiot, an accusation that is the product of lazy stereotyping; it is slanderous to confuse the Manly Man with an entirely different male demographic of gun-toting, Steven Segal-loving, 4x4 fetishists, known as gobshites. On the other hand, some sections of the media attempt to turn Manly support away from the environmental community by suggesting that tree-hugging ideologies only serve to justify tax hikes, get students laid and legitimize the sexual exploitation of trees.

Such manipulation will not work. Manly Men are not car-obsessed idiots who shower in petrol and eat half a cow for breakfast each morning. Sure, we all love Kit from *Knight Rider*, but we also know that unless you live on a farm or have a very

137

small penis, there is no real need for a 4x4. Manly Men cycle up mountains and then hang-glide from off the top in order to get a better view of the wonderful world in which they live. Sport and boobs are all very interesting, but we do occasionally glance from the sports section and page 3 to see what is going on in the world. The Manly Man knows that nothing is more noble or manly, than trying to save the world: protecting endangered animals and environments and jumping to the defence of the defenceless. The only thing more manly than driving a digger, is fighting one.

Manlifesto: The Manly Man knows that his own life and wellbeing are inextricably linked to those of plants, animals and the planet, itself. Life sees itself through our eyes and uses our bodies and minds to appreciate (and play with) itself; in reality, to love Nature is to love ourselves in a way that is only mildly onanistic.

London

William Blake

Ever since Puss'n Boots went off to seek his fortune and made a killing in junk bonds, only to blow it all on string, catnip and hookers, London has been a magnet of hope and ambition to all. People have bought into the fallacy that a life in 'The City', free from the tyranny of Wellington boots and Pac A Macs, is one of opportunity, affluence and culture. However, the reality for most city-dwellers is an unhappy life struggling to make ends meet in an un-natural environment.

Although William Blake wrote this poem about the social inequality and hardship of living in 18th Century London, it could just as easily have been written about any other metropolis, then or now. Cities continue to grow and have evolved into a new beast, the Megacity (population >10 000 000). People still flock to the city to find work and a better quality of life. Many people believe that, through the creation of cities, mankind has successfully bent the environment and the workplace to its will. In this poem, Blake reminds us that the stark truth is that people are bent to the will of the city and the people who run it. He urges the Manly Man to stand up against the horrors of city-living and social inequality, and has some useful advice for anybody tempted to dabble in a spot of harlotry.

London

I wander through each chartered street,
Near where the chartered Thames does flow,
And mark in every face I meet,

Marks of weakness, marks of woe.

In every cry of every man,
In every infant's cry of fear,
In every voice, in every ban,
The mind-forged manacles I hear:

How the chimney-sweeper's cry
Every blackening church appals,
And the hapless soldier's sigh
Runs in blood down palace-walls.

But most, through midnight streets I hear
How the youthful harlot's curse
Blasts the new-born infant's tear,
And blights with plagues the marriage-hearse.

Stanza 1

I wander through each chartered street,…Near where the chartered Thames does flow,….And mark in every face I meet,…Marks of weakness, marks of woe.

In stanza one, the poet walks through 18th century London and observes all that is going on around him. At this time, London was the capital of the most powerful country on earth; the centre of banking, fashion, government, royalty and religion; London was a Megacity that was the focus of wealth, prosperity, culture and all things 'Mega'. In fact, London was so Mega that it had long been favoured by Monarchs and was deemed worthy of its own charter.

Monarchs granted charters to some cities so that their populations could exercise special rights and privileges; however, only the favoured few had the power to do so, and it was usually at the expense of the ragged-trousered masses. The charter granted freedoms that were based upon rules and regulations designed to suit only the rich and powerful, and did little for the poor locals or immigrants that flocked to London for a better life.[97]

Throughout history, London has attracted workers from all over world with the giddy promise of jobs, safety in numbers and bright-red double-decker buses. The city casts these dreams, like the neon lure of an angler fish, guiding people into its concrete belly, before shutting its jaws tightly behind them. Dreams turn to ash in the industrial innards of the beast; and what people actually get is the nightmare of working long hours for low pay, a life in constant fear that someone will steal the front wheel of their bicycle and the exquisite irony of feeling so alone, amongst so many.[98]

The success of London is not reflected in the faces of its people, where William Blake sees weakness rather than strength, and sadness rather than happiness. The city has left a sorrowful mark upon its people like a scar.

Stanza 2

In every cry of every man,…In every infant's cry of fear,…In every voice, in every ban,…The mind-forged manacles I hear:

---

[97] Given the special dispensations and financial freedoms that 'The City' continues to enjoy today, it appears that little has changed; bankers are the new Royalty.
[98] Nowadays, our loneliness is made even more acute by the fact that we must listen to other people's mobile phone conversations during our commute; it would be tempting to shove their mobile phones up their arses, if we could be sure that it wouldn't just make it easier for them to talk shite.

The people of Blake's London are not happy chappies; the cheerful calls of the cockney stall holder and tap-dancing chimney sweep have been replaced by the fearful cries of a people oppressed by authority. People were controlled by 'bans', which were proclamations of the economic, religious and political powers of the time, laws designed to constrict the freedom of every man and keep the masses in their place. The success of the capital city is based on the laws of capitalism itself. It is also based on people buying into the lie that capitalism goes hand in hand with justice and democracy. We are trained from an early age to believe that market forces are objective and allow us to make decisions based upon hard facts and data; however, the numbers have always been stacked against the poor, and while the markets may be neutral, that just means they don't give a shit about Tiny Tim.

Stanza 3

How the chimney-sweeper's cry...Every blackening church appals,....And the hapless soldier's sigh...Runs in blood down palace-walls.

The language of this stanza sits uneasily with our rose-tinted, lamb-choppered idea of London's past; a romantic Dickensian worlde of happy-go-lucky street urchins and batty old women roaming about in their wedding dresses. However, this poem predates Dickens. It was written at the beginning of the industrial revolution, when London was expanding rapidly on a diet of greed and exploitation; a time when the chimney sweep was too busy working to have time to tuck his thumbs behind his braces and have a right old knees up.

The people of London are miserable, but their melancholic cries are ignored by the people in power, the Church and politicians, alike. Religious leaders are aware of the social inequality, but rather than act as a shining light of moral values, they have become blackened and polluted by the filthy by-products of industrial production and wealth. The enlightenment of Christian thinking has become grubby and sleazy (which is maybe not all that surprising for a credulous philosophy based on supernatural infidelity).[99]

The other main focus of authority is the state, which uses the threat of military action to enforce its rules and practices. At Buckingham Palace, we can go and see the uniformed soldiers in their brightly polished brass and shining leather, and appreciate the spectacle of the changing of the guards; however, we shouldn't forget that when these men and women are not posing in big fluffy hats on the front of shortbread tins, they are killing machines that have sworn to defend the Royal family against foreign enemies and middle-aged protestors dressed-up as Batman. Back in Blake's time, if you tried mooning the Queen, those 'friendly', furry-hatted fellows would have cleaved off your buttocks and had them impaled on spikes over London Bridge as a lesson to one and all.

So, the great city of London operates upon fear, exploitation and the threat of violence. But exploitation does not just come from the top, it runs right through this society from top to bottom.

Stanza 4

But most, through midnight streets I hear…How the youthful harlot's

---

[99] "Seriously, Joseph mate, I'm sorry. Mary said you guys were on a break," is not an acceptable excuse for a being that is supposed to be omnipotent.

curse...Blasts the new-born infant's tear,...And blights with plagues the marriage-hearse.

In the final stanza, Blake observes the brutal effect that city-living and capitalism have on love itself. *'The youthful harlot's curse'* is to sell her body to the highest bidder and the result is misery piled upon misery. We associate marriage with youth and happiness. We look to the future through the next generation and our hopes are with them. But what kind of future do they have when they are seen as just another industrial commodity? For the harlot, motherhood is the unhappy by-product of an economic transaction; it is cursed because it holds up business.

With the dawn of the Megacity has come Megaharlotry, whereby the body of a woman (generally, one in dire financial strife) can be rented out for nine months at a time. Embryos from rich women, who do not wish to have their bodies or careers inconvenienced by pregnancy, can be implanted in the wombs of surrogate mothers, who run the gauntlet of pregnancy, in exchange for a rental fee. Now, while that Manly Man respects a woman who takes a little pride in her appearance (a spot of makeup and fake tan perhaps), he has no time for women who voluntarily send their foetuses to boarding school for nine months, regardless of how firm it keeps their boobs.

With each line of the poem, a new horror is revealed, culminating in the mother reacting to her infant's tears with anger and resentment rather than love and sympathy. In the city of London, it is not only the buildings that are blackening, but the hearts of men and women. Here, even marriage is cursed to the grave, as the harlot *'blights with plagues the marriage-hearse'* by spreading venereal disease to men, and then on to their wives, so that marriage could mean a death sentence. In Blake's time,

144

sexually transmitted diseases had more serious consequences than an itchy ballbag and an embarrassing visit to the doctor.

The sad truth is that Blake's London operates through a system of social inequality and exploitation, underpinned by religious and political rules, with an ever present threat of violence not far below the surface. Good job things have changed so much since then..., *'hmmm'*.

At first glance, the problems associated with overpopulation that we face nowadays (at least in developed countries) are a world away from those that confronted Blake and his mates. An hour-long commute on an overcrowded train, with your head wedged between a sweat-stained armpit and a grime-stained window, is less inconvenient than, say, the threat of cholera or being raped by bandits on your way to work. Yet, despite all the advances in sanitation, security and technology, the faces that shuffle by in modern day London look as though someone has stolen the jelly out of their eels. Social inequality still exists and the inhabitants of today's Megacities are no less miserable than those of Blake's London.

According to the UN, *"Megacities are major global risk areas. Due to highest concentration of people and extreme dynamics, they are particularly prone to supply crises, social disorganization, political conflicts and natural disasters."*[100] Still, people seem to think that as long as you can get

---

[100] And more prone to having to deal with Megawankers; if a Megacity is an urban area with a population of over 10 000 000 and 1 in every 25 people is a wanker (and this is a conservative estimate), that's a whopping 400 000 Megawankers depleting reserves of goodwill and boxes of Kleenex. 400 000 idiots who talk loudly on their mobile phones during your train-journey and look down their nose at ignorant country-folk not clever enough to give up the vulgarity of natural daylight and fresh air for a 2-hour commute and the privilege of paying over the odds to live in a bedshit (not a spelling mistake).

a kebab at 03:00 in the morning, it's worth living somewhere shit…literally shit.

In London, rivers of excrement flow beneath the swanky boutiques and £1000 dresses of Oxford Street, and noxious gas bubbles beneath Buckingham Palace. Still it could be worse; Tokyo is a Super-Duper-Megacity that has a poop-ulation of around 37 000 000 people, each crapping out a 1.4 kg whopper every day (3 kg for Sumo wrestlers), so that the city squats upon 51 800 tonnes of shit. The only reason that Tokyo is not elevated to a great height by such a build-up of excrement is because it's all washed away by 50 700 000 litres of piss every twenty-four hours.

However, the worst part of living in the city is not the overcrowding or the pollution, it is the social inequality. The disparity in wealth between the 'haves' and the 'have nots' of this world, is even more exaggerated in the city. No more so than in London, where the homeless are kept awake not just by the cold, but the sound of gold-plated Ferraris being raced up and down the streets by the sons of rich sheiks. Studies have shown that everybody is less happy in an unequal society;[101] the poor resent the rich, while the rich worry that the poor will rise up against them and steal their gold-plated hub caps.

The Manly Man cannot sit idle in the face of such injustice and

---

[101] The Manly Man could do worse than familiarize himself with this excellent piece of research, which is summarized in a book called 'The Spirit Level'. The authors demonstrate and explain how people living in regions with greater inequality between rich and poor not only have lower life expectancy, but live in societies that are more violent and obese, and less shaggable, educated and trusting. By contrast, the research shows that economic equality benefits everybody, not just the poor; even rich people living in a more equal society (e.g. Sweden) live longer, sexier lives compared to those that live in an unequal society (e.g. USA; for more information visit www.equalitytrust.org.uk).

economic silliness. He knows that the problem of economic inequality will not be solved by raging against the rich and patronizing the poor; it is a matter of education. The Manly Man is committed to learning about how economic equality leads to happier, healthier and all-round sexier societies, and sharing the Good News with others. So, Manly Men unite! Go forth and do what you can to make the world a happier, safer and fairer place for all (preferably from the comfort of your tent in the country, rather than a sleeping bag under Westminster Bridge).

Manlifesto: The Manly Man knows that life for everyone is better in a more equal society; consequently, he judges himself and others by social rather than economic values (and how quickly they can down a pint). Above all, the Manly Man knows that only a wanker worries about pleasing themselves alone.

And in the Frosty Season… (Extract from The Prelude)

William Wordsworth

'*And in the Frosty Season…*' is an extract from *The Prelude*, an epic autobiographical poem and vanity project that Wordsworth wrote in order to prove his greatness as a poet and philosopher. Fortunately, in amongst the ego and the ambition there's some cracking poetry. Wordsworth believed that poetry was the expression of powerful emotions recollected in tranquillity. In this section of *The Prelude*, he puts this theory into practice to capture the powerful, emotional commune between Nature and Man and the feeling of '*Weeeeeeeeee!*' you get when wheeling about on ice skates.

Wordsworth reminds us that it's not only important to appreciate the present moment for the existential pleasure that it brings, but we should also attempt to etch the good times into our mind so that we can do justice to their memory in the future. He urges us to savour and record the fleeting beauty of the world so that we can inspire ourselves and others at a later date. So prepare to grab a pen and write down wintry memories of skating on the local duck pond or trying to light-up one of your dad's cigarettes while wearing those mittens that your mum had sown into your duffle coat…stick that on one of your Christmas cards and smoke it, Oxfam!

The Prelude

And in the frosty season, when the sun

148

Was set, and visible for many a mile
The cottage windows through the twilight blaz'd,
I heeded not the summons:--happy time
It was, indeed, for all of us; to me
It was a time of rapture! Clear and loud
The village clock toll'd six; I wheel'd about,
Proud and exulting, like an untired horse,
That cares not for its home.--All shod with steel,
We hiss'd along the polish'd ice, in games
Confederate, imitative of the chace
And woodland pleasures, the resounding horn,
The Pack loud bellowing, and the hunted hare.
So through the darkness and the cold we flew,
And not a voice was idle; with the din,
Meanwhile, the precipices rang aloud,
The leafless trees, and every icy crag
Tinkled like iron, while the distant hills
Into the tumult sent an alien sound
Of melancholy, not unnoticed, while the stars,
Eastward, were sparkling clear, and in the west
The orange sky of evening died away.

Not seldom from the uproar I retired
Into a silent bay, or sportively
Glanced sideway, leaving the tumultuous throng,
To cut across the image of a star
That gleam'd upon the ice: and oftentimes
When we had given our bodies to the wind,
And all the shadowy banks, on either side,
Came sweeping through the darkness, spinning still
The rapid line of motion; then at once
Have I, reclining back upon my heels,
Stopp'd short, yet still the solitary Cliffs

149

Wheeled by me, even as if the earth had roll'd
With visible motion her diurnal round;
Behind me did they stretch in solemn train
Feebler and feebler, and I stood and watch'd
Till all was tranquil as a dreamless sleep.

Lines 1-6

And in the frosty season, when the sun...Was set, and visible for many a mile...The cottage windows through the twilight blaz'd,...I heeded not the summons:--happy time...It was, indeed, for all of us; to me...It was a time of rapture!...

The first long sentence of this poem sets the scene. It is twilight and frost covers the landscape. The cottage fires and oil lamps are lit. The day's work in the fields is over and it is time to be inside, but the children ignore the summons to return home; they have been released from school and their chores, and for them, this a time when the landscape, emptied of adults, becomes their own and they exult in their freedom. The exclamation mark at the end of the first sentence emphasises their intense feeling of liberty, which borders on rapture.[102]

This is a scene of childhood innocence and joy that we all remember, somehow, despite never having skated upon a country pond at the beginning of the Industrial revolution in England. Before us, the poet unfurls a scene straight from one of those Oxfam Christmas cards that the mothers and girlfriends of Manly Men send to family and friends on their behalf; wintry compositions of snow-filled landscapes, burned orange and

---

[102] Religious joy; not a type of dinosaur.

brown by dead leaves and the latest woollen fashions of a bygone age.[103]

Lines 6-13

...Clear and loud... The village clock toll'd six; I wheel'd about,...Proud and exulting, like an untired horse,...That cares not for its home.--All shod with steel,...We hiss'd along the polish'd ice, in games...Confederate, imitative of the chace...And woodland pleasures, the resounding horn,...The Pack loud bellowing, and the hunted hare.

The lines of the next long sentence run together to describe the breathless excitement of the children as they twist and turn in the dizzy joy of the skating games. The line, *'All shod with steel, We hiss'd along the polish'd ice...'* is a great example of how words can be used to create the actual sound of the thing that they are describing. You can hear the sound of steel skates hissing on the ice. The joy of the activity sings through the whole sentence. The children are lost in a world of their imagination, chasing each other as hunter or hunted, playing together in a confederation of happy freedom.

Lines 14-22

So through the darkness and the cold we flew,...And not a voice was idle; with the din,...Meanwhile, the precipices rang aloud,...The leafless trees, and every icy crag...Tinkled like iron, while the distant hills...Into the tumult sent an alien sound...Of melancholy, not unnoticed, while the

---

[103] A classier, if less hilarious, reminder of Christmas than the cartoon of Santa lighting one of Rudolph's farts (in order to make his sleigh go faster) that many a Manly Man would have sent.

stars,…Eastward, were sparkling clear, and in the west…The orange sky of evening died away.

The children cry out with joy and laughter. The chorus of their voices strikes the cold air, and rings and echoes through the mountainous countryside; it reverberates off the icicles hanging from branches and rocks, which *'tinkled like iron'*, so that the landscape itself seems to join in the tumult of noise and activity.

But in the midst of it all the poet hears a different sound, perhaps the wind whistling through the trees or moaning through the hills. He looks beyond the immediacy of the children's game to the sad, silent hills in the distance and notices an unfamiliar tune upon the frosty air, *'an alien sound…Of melancholy, not unnoticed'*. The poet's thoughts turn from the hills to the vastness of the heavens above. As the light of the sun fades, something sinister melts into the last lines of the first section, like a well-placed snowball down the back of your neck; a note of melancholy is struck upon the frosty air.[104]

Lines 23-38

Not seldom from the uproar I retired…Into a silent bay, or sportively…Glanced sideway, leaving the tumultuous throng,…To cut across the image of a star…That gleam'd upon the ice: and oftentimes…When we had given our bodies to the wind,….And all the shadowy banks, on either side,…Came sweeping through the darkness, spinning still…The rapid line of motion; then at once…Have I, reclining back upon my heels,…Stopp'd

---

[104] Melancholy is not a word known to the snowball-throwing Childly Child of Christmas past. However, even children know subconsciously that all is transient, and this happy time may never return; which explains why it's so difficult to get the little buggers to come in for their dinner.

short, yet still the solitary Cliffs…Wheeled by me, even as if the earth had roll'd…With visible motion her diurnal round;…Behind me did they stretch in solemn train…Feebler and feebler, and I stood and watch'd…Till all was tranquil as a dreamless sleep.

In this final section of the poem, Wordsworth reminds us that he was always a bit special; even as a boy, he sought the peace and quiet in which to contemplate nature. Already, like the Manly Man he would become, the young Wordsworth in the poem has a keen appreciation of the world. He skates off with a sideways glance to leave the throng, sweeping through the frosty darkness.

Wordsworth creates a sense of movement that is immediate and infectious, we feel as if we are skating alongside him, feeling the wind on our face as we speed through a galaxy of stars. As the boy skates on, he is captivated by a shooting star reflected in the dark surface of the ice. In real-life this would be the moment, just when we think that all is well with the world, that we go arse over tit; however, the poet falls not on his arse, but into a transcendental awe.[105]

The mood of the poem suddenly changes as the boy is stopped short in the midst of his youthful exuberance; his skates hiss to a stop, but he feels the whole earth continue to move around him. He can no longer hear the shouts and cries of the other skaters; he is alone in the centre of the universe. At this moment he is fully alive and at one with the elemental forces

---

[105] It is fortunate that ice skating is not complicated further by ski-bikinis; it is ironic that Manly Men are more likely to trip and fall on the beach than on ice. Thankfully, but for a small group of muppet-loving fetishists there is nothing sexy about mittens or duffel coats. Winter fashions make Miss World look like the Honey Monster and it is to the Honey Monster's great injustice that a revealing swimsuit does not work the same magic in reverse.

around him. He is experiencing a moment of total sensation, a moment of almost religious intensity. [106]

The effect upon the boy is profound. The tumult has ended and his pulse slows to normal, the dizziness steadies and a sense of calmness settles over him; a tranquil joy infuses through his senses. The boy's rational self is asleep and he experiences, through pure sensation, a feeling of completeness that joins him with his companions, with the leafless trees, with the glassy landscape, with the earth and with the stars in the heavens. He is rooted to the spot in calm wonder at the magnificence of the universe.

As we share in the poet's moment of existential bliss, we are reminded of intense moments of happiness from our own childhood. Memories from the verses of our own personal history spark into life and light up our thoughts with brief moments of joy. And *that* is what makes this poem so personal and so worthy. It's almost enough to make you want to write an epic, autobiographical poem!

Although the Manly Man does his best to live in the present and appreciate each moment, he knows that you cannot conjure-up existential bliss at will; it requires discipline, time and effort. One of the best ways that you can increase your chances of experiencing a little existential bliss, legally, is to do a few

---

[106] This religious epiphany could perhaps explain why William Wordsworth was prescient enough to include the name of the world's greatest living Christian, Sir Cliff Richard in the line '*Stopp'd short, yet still the solitary Cliffs*'. The pope gets no mention, but there's Sir Cliff, sneaking in as always, to all things festive; a festive name muttered under the same mulled-wine scented sentence as Jesus Christ and Santa: "Jesus Christ, I wish Santa would bring Cliff Richard a lover so that he would have less free time to write music or sing."

lines...of writing... every day.[107] Scientists have shown that people who keep a diary, or take time to write about three things that went well during their day, are significantly happier than people who do not.[108]

The Manly Man knows that the act of regularly writing things down helps him to appreciate the little touches of class that make each day Manly and magnificent. These are the moments that we can string together into the epic poem of our own lives. So, write down some of the things that have made you feel good today and have a go at making them rhyme if you think you're man enough.[109]

Manlifesto: The Manly Man takes the time and effort to appreciate the here and now. Each day he reflects upon the things that make life worth living such as: the black gold-trimmed silhouette of the mountains against a bruised purple sky at sunrise; whizzing through the traffic jam on a bicycle on the way to work; and the sweet existential joy of receiving a free sample of cheese on a cocktail stick while doing the shopping.

---

[107] Writing a few lines every day is also a much cheaper alternative to snorting them.
[108] Seligman ME, Steen TA, Park N, Peterson C. Positive psychology progress: empirical validation of interventions. Am Psychol 2005;60:410-21.
[109] Starter ideas: 'Ode to a piece of toast'; 'Meditation on a Teenager Falling Off a Skateboard'; 'Sonnet No. 135: Swimming Lane All to Myself How I Love Thee So'.

Birches

Robert Frost

Well, here it is. Our last poem and the ultimate test of your Manly mind; an end of term exam to see what you have learned about poetry, even if all that you have learned is that no amount of explanation (and taking the piss) is going to make you like it any more.[110] In the unlikely event that you still don't really care for poetry, at least you will have gained more of an appreciation for it. *Birches* is a whopper of a poem that will test that appreciation to the limit; it is a fifty-nine-line-legged beast of a poem about the capacity of Nature to inspire and delight mankind, Manly or otherwise.

This poem was written by Robert Frost, a Manly Man who not only wrote about the natural world, but also farmed it; a poet who was not afraid to get his hands dirty and knew all about hard, physical graft.[111] Frost was also a self-confessed swinger with an unhealthy fixation with forests and birch trees. He knew that Nature is not just *"a wet place where large numbers of ducks fly by overhead uncooked"*,[112] but it is also a free resource with an infinite capacity to inspire creativity and happiness in all of us, from poets to plumbers.

This poem reminds the Manly Man that Nature is more than an immense outdoor playground with mountains to conquer and

---

[110] Although this is unlikely to be the case if you've made it this far…unless you are a seriously damaged. individual with a penchant for intellectual self-harm (in which case we refer you back to *Ode on Melancholy*)

[111] He also worried about never having enough time to get things done…important things…like picking apples (see *Apple Picking*).

[112] Quote from Oscar Wilde.

trees to climb. Nature is something to which we are inextricably linked and somewhere we can go in order to find a sense of peace and tranquillity. Scientific research shows that spending time in Nature makes us happier, kinder, more creative and muddier…poetry shows that it also makes us Manlier.

Birches

When I see birches bend to left and right
Across the lines of straighter darker trees,
I like to think some boy's been swinging them.
But swinging doesn't bend them down to stay.
Ice-storms do that. Often you must have seen them
Loaded with ice a sunny winter morning
After a rain. They click upon themselves
As the breeze rises, and turn many-coloured
As the stir cracks and crazes their enamel.
Soon the sun's warmth makes them shed crystal shells
Shattering and avalanching on the snow-crust
Such heaps of broken glass to sweep away
You'd think the inner dome of heaven had fallen.
They are dragged to the withered bracken by the load,
And they seem not to break; though once they are bowed
So low for long, they never right themselves:
You may see their trunks arching in the woods
Years afterwards, trailing their leaves on the ground,
Like girls on hands and knees that throw their hair
Before them over their heads to dry in the sun.
But I was going to say when Truth broke in
With all her matter-of-fact about the ice-storm,

I should prefer to have some boy bend them
As he went out and in to fetch the cows--
Some boy too far from town to learn baseball,
Whose only play was what he found himself,
Summer or winter, and could play alone.
One by one he subdued his father's trees
By riding them down over and over again
Until he took the stiffness out of them,
And not one but hung limp, not one was left
For him to conquer. He learned all there was
To learn about not launching out too soon
And so not carrying the tree away
Clear to the ground. He always kept his poise
To the top branches, climbing carefully
With the same pains you use to fill a cup
Up to the brim, and even above the brim.
Then he flung outward, feet first, with a swish,
Kicking his way down through the air to the ground.
So was I once myself a swinger of birches.
And so I dream of going back to be.
It's when I'm weary of considerations,
And life is too much like a pathless wood
Where your face burns and tickles with the cobwebs
Broken across it, and one eye is weeping
From a twig's having lashed across it open.
I'd like to get away from earth awhile
And then come back to it and begin over.
May no fate willfully misunderstand me
And half grant what I wish and snatch me away
Not to return. Earth's the right place for love:

I don't know where it's likely to go better.
I'd like to go by climbing a birch tree
And climb black branches up a snow-white trunk
Toward heaven, till the tree could bear no more,
But dipped its top and set me down again.
That would be good both going and coming back.
One could do worse than be a swinger of birches.

Lines 1-4

When I see birches bend to left and right...Across the lines of straighter darker trees,....I like to think some boy's been swinging them...But swinging doesn't bend them down to stay.

Robert Frost delivers this poem in a conversational way, as if he were talking to a friend and knew that this poem would one day find its way into the hands of a fellow Manly Man, such as yourself. In the first sentence, Frost contrasts the appearance of the straight dark pine trees with that of the hunch-backed birches, whose boughs and branches arch away from their trunks and down towards the earth; he imagines that the branches of the birches have been bent and bowed by the weight of some boy clambering and swinging upon them. However, Frost quickly dispels this romantic notion and acknowledges that the trees could not have been permanently damaged by a single boy's adventuring (no matter how portly the little fellow). These opening lines of the poem tell us that even though poet has a vivid imagination, he does not have his head in the clouds; there is clearly a conflict between his poetic and pragmatic visions of the world.

Lines 5-9

Ice-storms do that. Often you must have seen them...Loaded with ice a sunny winter morning...After a rain. They click upon themselves...As the breeze rises, and turn many-coloured...As the stir cracks and crazes their enamel.

The poet tells us in simple, practical language that ice storms are the real reason why the branches of the birch trees stay bent; they have been bowed and broken by their environment. The stunted trees have been pulled and beaten into shape by relentless gales and the burden of ice. This is just one example of the power of Nature; all around us, environmental forces exert their will on people and places: the broken blood vessels on the weather-beaten face of a fisherman, the calloused hands and broken backs of women working in rice fields, or the bright-pink sheen of a freshly sunburned football hooligan.

Lines 10-13

Soon the sun's warmth makes them shed crystal shells...Shattering and avalanching on the snow-crust...Such heaps of broken glass to sweep away...You'd think the inner dome of heaven had fallen.

The poet is not distracted by the cold, rather his thoughts are focused by it. His poetic mind conjures an image of crystalline beauty from the wintry world around him. Meanwhile, the rest of us are calculating the cost of a trip to Barbados, as we scratch the ice of the windscreen of our car with a credit card, praying that the engine still starts.

Most men can appreciate beauty, but few can express it adequately. Faced with the image of sunlight on snow, most men would be satisfied with, 'That snow looks class, all white and sparkly, like.' Or, at a push, "I say old bean, the landscape appears as though it were dusted with icing sugar and cocaine, what?" However, Frost raises the bar with a tactic that can be used to devastating effect at the bar: a little poetic observation about the world around you. The Manly Man knows that there's nothing like a bit of existentialist, living-for-the-moment, observation to impress the ladies, confuse the dandies, and make you feel all at-one-ly with the world.

Marketing folk use poetic language and sparks of fantasy all the time to connect with us and entice us into buying their products. Guinness, which essentially tastes like a pint of evil, would be difficult to swallow had we not already swallowed the mythology that 'Guinness gives us strength'[113] and is made from a careful blend of Celtic legend and organic Leprechaun milk. With this subtle spin and hocus pocus of perspective, Guinness is simply the most Manly drink a dreamer can order (much of the fantasy lies in the idea that it is worth £4.50 a pint).

Likewise, you can market your mind as a splendid place, furnished with profound insights, rather than a mechanism for checking whether or not the object before you can be screwed, eaten, or safely ignored.

Lines 14-20

They are dragged to the withered bracken by the load,....And they seem not to break; though once they are bowed...So low for long, they never right themselves:...You may see their trunks arching in the woods...Years

---

[113] The only things Guinness gives you are particularly interesting and vigorous trips to the bathroom the next day; although with practice, Guinness does taste great.

afterwards, trailing their leaves on the ground,...Like girls on hands and knees that throw their hair...Before them over their heads to dry in the sun.

Here, the poet describes the practicalities of clearing up the broken birches after the ice storm; but still his mind wanders from the truth before him to the fantasies it conjures. Just like the trees themselves, his thoughts begin to branch out as he takes in the wonder of what he sees. The great glass dome of the skies has shattered into pieces and fallen to earth. The boughs of the birches have been dragged down under the weight of the ice until they make contact with the barren soil. Although the tall straight pines point directly to heaven, they are broken by the harsh winter. In contrast, the birches strain to grow heavenward but their branches make contact with the ground; they are in a state of balance between heaven and earth.

Nature inspires thought after thought in the poet's mind, so that the stooped bodies and flowing branches of the birches look *'like girls on hands and knees that throw their hair before them over their heads to dry in the sun'*.[114] Once again, the poet is on the point of being carried away by his imagination...but then the *'truth broke in'*.

Lines 21-22

But I was going to say when Truth broke in...With all her matter-of-fact about the ice-storm,...

In these lines, the poet uses a capital T to personify Truth.[115]

---

[114] A similar idea is used by Keats in his poem *Ode To Autumn*.

[115] As you now know, this is a common device that allows poets to talk about abstract ideas and things as if they were real people; Philip Larkin and John Keats were big fans of using capital letters to magic Time and Melancholy into life (see *Send no Money* and *Ode on Melancholy*).

Truth is female and she breaks into the poet's thoughts to interrupt his flight of imagination; we can all relate to that moment when she bursts in uninvited. Truth is nowhere to be found when you're looking for weapons of mass destruction, but have a drunken snog with your high-school piano teacher and Truth leaps in, heroically, teeth gleaming and cape fluttering in the wind. And all you want is for Truth to f*ck away off and let you have this minor indiscretion. There are elections being rigged, child soldiers being exploited, and nuclear weapons being developed. So for Christ's sake, let the 17-year-old into the nightclub with his fake ID or permit some other white lie that makes the world a little more beautiful…like maybe the birches were bent by a boy swinging on them.

The truth is that the birches have been bowed and bent by the weight of ice, but wouldn't it be great if there was a more fantastical explanation[116] that didn't have to be explained by somebody with sensible glasses and brown suede patches on the elbows of their corduroy blazer?

Lines 23-32

I should prefer to have some boy bend them…As he went out and in to fetch the cows--….Some boy too far from town to learn baseball,…Whose only play was what he found himself,…Summer or winter, and could play alone….One by one he subdued his father's trees…By riding them down over and over again…Until he took the stiffness out of them,….And not one but hung limp, not one was left…For him to conquer. He learned all there was…

The poet's thoughts return to the boy swinging on the branches

---

[116] It's more entertaining to think that the sound of thunder is really God doing burpees and squat-jumps on a celestial wooden floor.

of the birches and he reminisces about childhood. The boy has no playmates living near, so when his daily chores on the farm are done he has to create his own sources of adventure and entertainment. And what better excitement for a boy (and a Manly Man if we're being honest) than climbing trees and swinging off their branches? This pastime is an act of defiance against his daily chores and his father's authority. The boy is a hero. Like Don Quixote charging at windmills, he has created and bested his own adversaries. One by one, he has subdued and birch-slapped each mighty tree until none are left unconquered. The branches of all the birch trees have been brought down in limp subjection to their master!

Lines 33-40

To learn about not launching out too soon…And so not carrying the tree away…Clear to the ground. He always kept his poise…To the top branches, climbing carefully…With the same pains you use to fill a cup…Up to the brim, and even above the brim….Then he flung outward, feet first, with a swish,…Kicking his way down through the air to the ground.

Anybody who has seen an episode of *You've Been Framed*[117] will appreciate that there is a certain amount of skill to swinging about on birch trees. The boy in the poem has mastered this important life skill. He has learned that if you swing on a branch that is too low you will hit the ground. If you swing from a branch that is too high you stay up in the air. The right balance is found by trial and error, like working out how many drinks you can carry back from the bar without spilling a drop. The result is a controlled leap of faith, filled with danger and excitement.

---

[117] Cheaply made UK TV program comprised of 'hilarious' home videos of people falling off tyre swings into wedding cakes.

The poet makes us reflect on how easily amused we were as children, fascinated by simple activities that we now take for granted. When did it stop being fun to splash around in a puddle? Since when were metre sticks used to measure stuff, rather than fight pirates? Remember lying beside your bicycle in the middle of the road, giving the wheel a quick spin every now and then, to make it look as if you had just fallen off? A car slows down to offer you assistance, but you are up like a flash and, after a two fingered salute, the chase is on!

It is a sad fact that these feats of childhood 'daring do' are replaced by the 'better nots' of adulthood as we grow older. It's worth bearing this in mind before criticising the youth of today, who have swapped tree bending for thumb-twiddling on game-consoles. The sad truth is that most adults have lost the power to amuse themselves without God, a set of golf clubs, or too much to drink.

Lines 41-47

So was I once myself a swinger of birches.....And so I dream of going back to be.....It's when I'm weary of considerations,....And life is too much like a pathless wood...Where your face burns and tickles with the cobwebs...Broken across it, and one eye is weeping...From a twig's having lashed across it open.

Excellent going! We have reached line forty-one of the poem. It has been hard graft, but our breathing is regular and we have yet to cramp up. Manly determination dictates that we must see out this marathon. In this section, Frost dreams of being a boy again. As a boy he had poise and balance. His childhood innocence allowed him to take risks. He could make the leap and feel alive. Now, as an adult, he wants to recapture that sense of wonder and thrill. The daily grind of adult responsibilities has led him into a dense thicket where he can no longer see where he is going; a place where everything seems to conspire against him and hold him back in a tangle of tasks, duties and the mundane business of getting through each day.

Fortunately, Manly Men recognise this daily disillusion and we have swapped our pin-striped suits for trivial pursuits: paint-balling, mountain climbing, abseiling, go-karting, and other activities where we pay large sums of money to be pulled and propelled in all sorts of directions (and not just in a naughty way). It is the Manly Man's mission to help others recapture a childlike enjoyment of life and remind the ladies in his life to hop their scotch every now and again. [118]

Lines 48-49

I'd like to get away from earth awhile...And then come back to it and begin over.

The poet longs to escape to a place where he can rise above the confusion of earthly troubles. Somewhere he can go to for just a while, until he finds the strength to begin again. The ultimate place of escape from earthly troubles would be heaven, but to go there we would, of course, first have to die. The poet makes it clear that he does not long for death.

Lines 50-59

May no fate willfully misunderstand me...And half grant what I wish and

---

[118] It's hardly fair that while men are free to pursue the same activities they enjoyed playing as boys in the playground (such as football, obstacle course racing, battle re-enactment and board games), women don't nip out for a quick game of hopscotch or patty-cakery...or perhaps they have better things to do.

snatch me away...Not to return. Earth's the right place for love:...I don't know where it's likely to go better....I'd like to go by climbing a birch tree...And climb black branches up a snow-white trunk...Toward heaven, till the tree could bear no more,...But dipped its top and set me down again....That would be good both going and coming back....One could do worse than be a swinger of birches.

In the final section, the poet recognizes that this earthly life is precious and should not be wished away in the hope of some future heavenly existence. We are all faced with worries and obstacles as we beat a path through the tangled undergrowth of our lives, but the poet recognises that it is only here on this earth, that love on a human level can be found. Despite the imperfection and weariness associated with everyday life, it is here and now that we have the chance to love and be loved. There is magic in the mundane and love in the soil if we look for it. This is the branch we must grasp at; this is the leap of faith we must make!

Robert Frost reminds us that, just like the boy in the tree, we have to navigate life with skill and dexterity. Life is a great balancing act, in which we teeter between innocence and experience, imagination and reality, and freedom and responsibility. Whenever life seems complicated and overwhelming, Frost urges us to take solace and inspiration from nature and childhood. When life seems joyless and bleak, reconnecting with nature can help us to rekindle an existential appreciation for the here and now; you could do worse than swing on a birch tree to get your mojo back!

Manly Men are modern knights of chivalry; we brandish our metre sticks at boredom and apathy, and charge into life with saucepans on our heads and biscuit-tin shields held high. To us, the mundane is an alien concept that exists only in the thoughts of the limp-willed and floppy-minded. We have learned from the wisdom of poetry and are bound by our honour to use this knowledge to improve our lives and the lives of others. The world is a brilliant place, and poems are there to remind and reconnect us should we ever forget; they distil all of life's wonder and experience in order to motivate, inspire, console, and guide us along the path to Manliness. Now, whose round is it?!

Manlifesto: The Manly Man has his head in the clouds and his feet on the ground. He is both a dreamer and a pragmatist who balances his desires with his responsibilities. The Manly Man knows that everyday life is a gift and his biggest responsibility is to look for the magic in the mundane and share it with others. When life feels grubby, and we are world-wearied and overwhelmed by work, we should look to nature for inspiration; the only thing better than climbing a tree to get a healthier perspective on things, is swinging about on one!

Acknowledgements

This book has been many years in development and would not have been possible without the patience and encouragement of our family and friends. So, many thanks to our partners and life-muckers, Linda Craig and Connie McGrath, for their relentless enthusiasm and encouragement. To Niall Meehan for reading (and proof-reading) this book so thoroughly, with a special blend of bonhomie and pedantic glee. Thank you to Lindsay Judge and Andy Shepherd for their content editing and advice on the first few chapters; this advice paved the way for the format and style of the rest of the book.

Special thanks also go to the 'Manly Men' (and Womanly Women) who provided feedback on the book synopsis: Colin Downey, Brett Patterson, Gavin Bates, Danilo McGarry, Pete Alexander, Sara and Paul McGrillen, Stephen Moore and Barry McGrath. Finally, thanks to Niall 'Pulsar' McKeown and Helmut Elstner for beers and humouring Stephen's long lecturers and excuses regarding why this book was so important and why it has taken so long to write. We are also grateful to Drew McWilliams for advice on publishing and putting the blurb together.

Lastly, thanks to the rest of our frabjous family, Sarah, Anthony, Max and Isabel, for their support, cake-based counselling and all-round 'do-you-heart-good-ery'.

It goes without saying that we owe much to the poets whose works are included in this book; not only for creating such gems of beauty and wisdom that we were compelled to share them with others, but for providing the inspiration we needed to develop and finish the *Manly Book of Poems,* itself. We would like to acknowledge and thank the all the permissions agents and estates for permission to publish the copyrighted poems below.

Printed in Great Britain
by Amazon

81981559R00097